Contents

Opposite: The Old Brewery in 1958, decorated to
celebrate The Commonwealth Games in Cardiff.

Our special thanks to:

The late **Miss Jennifer Brain**, Great Granddaughter of J.B. Brain for her authorship of the 1982 Centenary booklet, without which this work would not have been possible.

Brian Glover, author, for his extraordinary knowledge of the history of our company and the Welsh brewing industry.

Stewart Dobson, Head of Marketing at Brains, for all his hard work in managing the project.

Gavin Dando, photographer, for photography of our current pub estate and items from our archive.

Brian Lee for permission to use photography from his book The Illustrated History of Cardiff's Pubs (also published by Breedon Books).

Huw Evans for the back cover photograph and other photography of the Welsh rugby team.

Celf Design and Clinic, the design agencies who have helped create, source and provide many images.

Narberth Museum for the James Williams images.

Foreword

As Group Chairman and together with John Rhys Non-Executive Director of S. A. Brain & Company Ltd., it is with great pleasure that we have been working on this book with Brian Glover over the past six months or so. We are both immensely proud of the achievements of the company founded by our Great and Great Great Grandfathers respectively over the past 125 years.

There have been many highlights since 1882 and as you will see from the pages of this book, the company has faced some significant threats to its future over the years, such as the temperance movement of the late 19th Century and the predatory advances of the UK's National Brewers in the 1960s and 70s.

However, we have remained strong and committed to retaining our independence. Along the way we have joined forces with some of the other famous names in the Welsh brewing and licensed trade business. These names include Buckleys of Llanelli, United Clubs Brewery of Pontyclun, who themselves had merged when we acquired them in 1997, and later James Williams of Narberth and Stedmans of Caerleon. Consequently, for completeness, this book covers the heritage of some of these companies, as well as the proud history of S.A. Brain & Company, which have made us the leading brewer and pub operator in Wales.

The book does not always follow a strict chronological order as for some aspects it makes more sense to review our involvement in them over the fullness of time. We have designed it to be as visual as possible, so that it can be enjoyed in detail when read through fully or in outline when flicked through more superficially. Either way, we hope you enjoy the book that has been designed to give you an insight into our unique and colourful history.

We are immensely proud of our company and the excellent shape it is in today and look forward to the next 125 years of independence, challenges and achievements.

Christopher M. Brain DL
Group Chairman and Great Grandson of
Joseph Benjamin Brain, Co-Founder

John F.W. Rhys
Non-Executive Director and Great Great Grandson of
Samuel Arthur Brain, Co-Founder

When I think of Brains..................

Rhodri Morgan, First Minister, Welsh Assembly Government
'Cardiff, the former coal-mining valleys of South Wales and the whole of Wales have changed hugely over the past quarter century.

So much of what everyone took for granted over the previous century in terms of jobs, social habits and the environment has altered out of all recognition since the 1980s.

Cardiff was full of dockers and steel workers who drank Brains, usually Dark. The Valleys were full of coal miners who didn't. They drank plenty, but not Brains.

North of Merthyr was another country, where people rarely went to Cardiff let alone into Cardiff pubs. However often they might see 'It's Brains You Want' on railway viaducts, they wouldn't order a pint of Brains to save their lives. Brains was for the denizens of Cardiff and no-one else. 'You can't give away a pint of Brains in Newport' was the mantra. That was the measuring rod of how parochial we in Wales were.

Personally I absorbed Brains through my skin in the 1940s by attending the Sunday School at the Hayes Tabernacl Welsh Baptist Chapel, which backed onto The Old Brewery. As the mash was fermenting next door, its heady odour would drift over the gravestones through the windows into the vestry and the chapel.

No wonder I took to it like a duck to water, when I reached drinking age. But then I am Cardiff born and bred.

The big question for Brains was how you convert a local product into a Welsh brand? If Welsh products stay parochial, they go nowhere. If they can spread the message from 300,000 people to 3 million people you can stay in business and grow the business.

That is what Brains have achieved. When you think of all the missed opportunities to promote high quality Welsh food and drink products to a wider audience, you have to give credit to those companies like Brains who decided to front up, face the challenge and step up to the plate.

Hey why am I using American baseball slang like 'step up to the plate' when I'm talking about Brains beer? I should use the proper Cardiff expression 'toe the pegs' – or is that being parochial again?'

Lord Kinnock of Bedwelty, Head of the British Council, former European Commissioner
'If Rioja is liquid sunshine, Brains Beer – SA, Bitter or Dark – is liquid Wales. It is like sipping silk.'

Peter Hain, Secretary of State for Wales
'As a real ale lover, a pint of legendary Brains SA really does evoke the pride and passion of Wales for me. It is the ideal accompaniment to the Bread of Heaven! My wife Elizabeth, meanwhile, will always order a glass of velvety-smooth Brains Dark whenever it is available at the bar.'

Ryan Jones, Wales Rugby International, British and Irish Lion
'For me, any celebration starts with a pint of SA!'

Aled Jones, Singer, Actor & Broadcaster
'I never feel happier at the end of a long week than when I have had that first pint of Brains to start the weekend.'

Martin Bayfield, Broadcaster, England Rugby International, British and Irish Lion
'Playing in Wales as an Englishman always meant a degree of discomfort. If we won, we got grief, if we lost, we got grief – so post match, we would make our way to the bar, order infinite amounts of SA and then make for the Severn Bridge as quickly as was humanly possible!'

Dame Tanni Grey-Thompson DBE
'I used to train past the brewery in Cardiff and you would always know when it was a brewing day because you could smell it from about a mile away.... it made me quite proud to think that it happened in Cardiff. If I talk to anyone who has been to Cardiff (especially on International Day), they usually ask about Brains. Then there was always the post match visit to the pub and a bag of chips from Caroline Street. Although Cardiff has changed so much over the years it is a wonderful memory that I have.... especially if we had beaten England!!!'

John Inverdale, TV presenter & Journalist
'One of my proudest personal achievements was passing my 100 words a minute shorthand test at journalism college in Cardiff. Only four of us from the group passed at the first time of asking, and we'd promised ourselves a night in The Old Arcade in the centre of the city if we achieved this notable landmark. The results duly came that afternoon, and we all headed off to town, certificates in hand. In those days the licencing laws were very different and we stood in the pouring rain outside the pub, for fully 20 minutes, waiting for the doors to open at six. At 30 seconds past six, the first pint of SA was poured, and a beer never tasted so good. As a regular visitor to Cardiff ever since, whether on international days or not, a pint of Brains is an essential part of the trip.'

Tom Shanklin, Wales Rugby International, British and Irish Lion
'I worked for Brains as an ambassador visiting customers and consumers across Wales. On my travels I learnt how Brains reflects the passion and pride of the Welsh nation. One perk, was being able to sample the beer they produce for free.'

Ieuan Evans, Broadcaster, Wales Rugby International, British and Irish Lion
'Brains is a little taste of real Wales; strong and silent, but treat it with respect otherwise it will leave you a little battle weary.'

Welsh Ale

When Alfred Barnard visited Brains Brewery in the late 19th Century, as part of his research for his monumental four-volume work *Noted Breweries of Great Britain and Ireland (1889-1891)*, there was one question trembling on his lips.

Once he was introduced to the head brewer, Mr G.J. Gard, he had to raise the issue. As the visitors obtained their first view of the new brewhouse, at the mashing stage, he needed to know. He could not contain himself any longer, even though he feared being rebuffed.

He recalled in his book, 'Calling the brewer's attention to the process, we wooed him cautiously to tell us how Welsh beer was made - that ambrosial liquor which was so dear to the hearts of our ancestors.'

Mr Gard, who was eager to show his eminent visitors his shining new plant, quickly dismissed the question, telling them that 'the old style of Welsh brewing has long since been abandoned in favour of the London and Burton processes, which produce a better flavoured and purer beverage, and most certainly a less heady one.'

BRAGAWD REVIVED

In 1994 a former Brains brewer, Iain Turnbull of Abertridwr, briefly tried to revive commercial production of bragawd, using a recipe from the Duke of Beaufort. The dark ruby-red brew contained honey and a blend of herbs and spices. It was double fermented and matured in oak casks for a year.

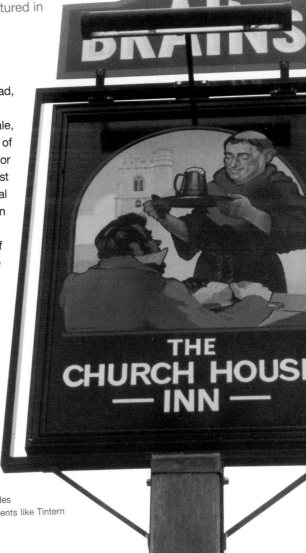

But what was that 'ambrosial liquor' which so intrigued Barnard? The 'heady brew' may have been lost in the steam of brewing progress, but its memories were still potent centuries later.

For Welsh ale was once highly-prized. When King Ine of Wessex in Southern England drew up a set of laws between 690 and 693AD, one of them referred to payments in kind in return for leasing land. The law ruled that for every 10 hides, the food rent should include '12 ambers of Welsh ale and 30 ambers of clear ale'.

Records of the Saxon period regularly divide ale into clear and Welsh. The latter did not need to come from Wales, but was a recognised native style driven West by the invading Saxons and then welcomed back into England when its intoxicating flavour was appreciated by the new rulers.

It was much more valuable than clear ale, being a heavy brew laced with expensive spices, like cinnamon, cloves and ginger, and sometimes herbs and honey. This was before hops were introduced into brewing in Britain in the 15th Century. Also known as bragawd or bragot, Welsh ale was second only to that other famous Celtic brew mead, made from fermented honey.

While most households brewed ale, richer bragawd tended to be a speciality of the nobles, the better taverns and the major brewers of the age – the monasteries. Most religious settlements boasted substantial brewhouses, like The Friary at Carmarthen or Tintern Abbey in the Wye Valley.

Henry VIII brought this holy alliance of brewing and the bible to an end when he dissolved the monasteries in 1536, at a time when the hop was leaping over other ingredients as the main flavouring in beer.

Bragawd passed into legend. It became the drink of giants. Gog and Magog, it was claimed, grew to their monstrous size on draughts of the brew. And it was still such a tantalising tale in Victorian Cardiff to intoxicate Barnard's imagination on his visit to Brains Brewery.

Brains' pub sign at The Church House Inn, St Brides Wentloog, reflects the fact that religious settlements like Tintern Abbey, above, once brewed their own beer.
Far left: Carreg Cennen.

As Cardiff expanded, so the brewery changed hands at a rapid rate

The Old Brewery

Cardiff may have celebrated its 100th anniversary as a city and its 50th as the capital of Wales in 2005, but until the 19th Century it was little more than a huddle of houses and inns around a decaying castle. In the census of 1801 it recorded a population of 1,870, which meant it had grown little since it was a Roman fort and then a Norman seat of power, commanding the lowest crossing point on the River Taff.

There was little industry and brewing for sale was confined to the backs of inns. The first Cardiff trade directory, *Bird's* of 1796, lists 18 pubs but no wholesale brewers, and just six maltsters and hop factors supplying the raw ingredients. The first common brewer, James Walters, mentioned in *Ridd's Directory* of 1813, was an extension of a malting business. His address in 1822 was St Mary Street, and he was brewing on the site of what became Brains Old Brewery.

As Cardiff expanded through the torrent of coal and iron cascading into the ancient borough from the valleys, thanks to the opening of the Glamorgan Canal in 1798 and then the Taff Vale Railway to Merthyr in

1841, so the brewery changed hands at a rapid rate. Edward Thomas Bridgen Carter was in charge by 1829. In 1835 the business was being run by Watson and Phillips, in 1840 by Phillips and Andrews and by 1844 by William and Charles Andrews, the latter for the first time using the title The Old Brewery. Part of the buildings dated back to 1713, from a date above a doorway.

By then the owners felt that they needed to emphasise that it was the town's original major ale producer, as The Old Brewery faced an increasing number of rivals in the Victorian boom town. *Hunt's Directory* of 1848 lists six common brewers. And the great thirst for beer continued to grow. The population rocketed to 41,400 by 1861 and doubled to 82,700 just 20 years later, as more docks were built to deliver the dusty black gold from Welsh mines to the world.

The new competitors cast envious eyes over 'The Old Brewery', for it was supplied with excellent well water despite being perilously close to a bulging bend in the River Taff. When William Williams, who had established Cardiff's second commercial brewery further up St Mary Street, had a chance to take over the original brewery he seized it, becoming the owner by 1848 and abandoning his own site.

Soon the highly-prized brewery changed hands again. By 1858 it was being run by Frederick Prosser, advertising himself as a beer and porter brewer, maltster, hop merchant and wine and spirits importer, as well as a supplier of bottled ales and stout. But when he died at an early age in 1860, the tragedy gave another rival brewer his chance.

John Thomas had established The New Brewery in Great Frederick Street by 1840, but once The Old Brewery came on the market he snapped it up in 1862 and gave it to his sons. John Griffen Thomas and Edward Inkerman Thomas traded as Thomas Brothers, developing a chain of 'retail establishments' including the famous Golden Cross and Old Arcade.

But it was their sister, Frances Elizabeth, who made the most significant connection when in 1872 she married Samuel Arthur Brain, who was to brand his name and initials on the rolling barrel of Cardiff beer.

The original Old Brewery, left, was little more than a three-storey stone building behind The Albert pub. Right: Local advertising in 1963 celebrated 250 years of The Old Brewery site.

Cardiff owed its expansion to the coal flowing through the port.

IMPERIAL LINKS

One of The Old Brewery's 19th Century owners, Frederick Prosser, typified the changing face of Cardiff. He was a young, well-travelled merchant. He had married the daughter of an army officer, Maria Adams, while in India, and their daughter, Adeline, was born in The Old Brewery in 1859. But his career was cruelly cut short when he died the following year while on a ship to India.

John Griffen Thomas threw down his pen and exclaimed 'Anarchy'. He resolved to sell up

First Brain Wave

Samual Arthur Brain was already well established in the beer business in Cardiff, since arriving in the town in the early 1860s as a young lad. He trained as a brewer and rose to be the manager of Dowson Brothers' Phoenix Brewery in Working Street, one of the growing number of new breweries in the mushrooming town.

Later, this brewery, with 15 pubs and a maltings in Cowbridge Road, was bought by Brains' arch rival in Cardiff William Hancock's, who adopted the phoenix as its symbol for almost 40 years. But it was S. A. Brain who had made the firebird's trade take off. Now he intended to fire up The Old Brewery.

He was descended from an eminent Gloucestershire family. His grandfather, William Brain of Kingswood, had been one of the leading mining engineers in the early 19th century. In 1822, with Aaron and Moses Brain, he had leased the Kingswood Colliery in Bristol from the Duke of Beaufort. This mining background meant the family had a keen interest in the much larger coalfields being developed in South Wales.

Joseph Benjamin Brain, far right, was a formidable financial figure who had rescued the grand West of England Bank, left, in Bristol, when it had collapsed in 1878. Samuel Arthur Brain, right, provided the brewing expertise in the founding partnership.

LEADING LIGHT

Joseph Benjamin Brain had wide business interests outside brewing. In 1888 he was also deputy chairman of the Bristol United Gas Light Company, which became the Bristol Gas Company in 1891.

The family were also into banking. Moses Brain even issued his own pound notes at one time under the name of Jones, Brain, Budgett & Co of Kingswood Hill.

S. A. Brain's father, Samuel Brain, was one of 12 children. His uncle, Joseph Benjamin Brain of Clifton, near Bristol, was the youngest, born in 1831. He was not only a man of substance – he was also a substantially reassuring figure when a major crisis hit the banking world in Bristol.

The West of England and South Wales District Banking Company had been established in Bristol in 1834. In 1857 the bank opened an opulent new head office in Corn Street, built in high Renaissance style. Its design was said to be based on the Library of St Mark in Venice, with high columns, arched windows and many relief figures. But was it pride before a crash?

In 1878 the company, which had 42 branches, collapsed with liabilities of £5 million, a vast sum at the time. 'This terrible catastrophe brought ruin to many hundreds of people,' said C.H. Cave in his *History of Banking in Bristol*.

Joseph Benjamin Brain stepped in to rescue what could be saved from the wreckage, helping to form the Bristol and West of England Bank the following year and becoming the new company's chairman. This bank, which had two branches in Cardiff, was taken over by Lloyds in 1892.

S. A. Brain went into partnership with this formidable financial figure, his uncle, to buy The Old Brewery in 1882 – with a little help from the temperance movement. For in 1881 the dry campaigners had succeeded in forcing the Welsh Sunday Closing Act through Parliament.

According to legend, John Griffen Thomas, who was then the sole owner of the brewery, on hearing the bitter news, threw down his pen and exclaimed 'Anarchy'. He resolved to sell up – and who better to buy him out than his brother-in-law S.A. Brain?

However, there are others who offer a simpler reason as to why Thomas was anxious to pull out. They say he was sliding into bankruptcy having invested heavily in the rush to buy up pubs. The Sunday Closing Act, which would stop trade on one of the busiest days of the week, was the final straw.

So Joseph Benjamin Brain and his nephew were not only taking over the oldest brewery in Cardiff, they were also taking on a huge challenge – to make the business succeed in difficult and hostile conditions.

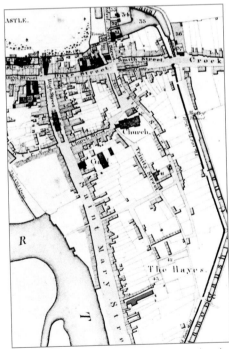

Early map of Cardiff, showing The Old Brewery in red.

Sunday Strife

As the pubs shut, so the shebeens – illegal drinking dens – opened

BUT I'VE LEARNT TO LOVE
MY ENEMIES!
On m'a appris à aimer mes ennemis.

It is impossible today to realise the strength of feeling generated in Wales by the temperance movement and its abhorrence of alcohol in the 19th Century. Led by the non-conformist churches, it became a religion in its own right, with many thousands signing the pledge.

Leading figures in Cardiff backed the fervent movement. Local shipping magnate John Cory had supported the founding of a Cardiff Total Abstinence Society as early as 1836. Later the Cory Memorial Temperance Hall was built opposite Queen Street railway station as a towering tribute to his commitment.

The Old Brewery could never ignore the issue. In fact, it was right in its face. An extensive symbol of the stern stand against intoxicating drink was erected right outside its front door. Temperance Town was built on land reclaimed from the River Taff between 1858 and 1864, street after street of houses with no pubs after landowner Colonel Wood had insisted that no 'tavern keeper, alehouse keeper or retailer of beer' be allowed. The main building was Wood Street Temperance Hall (later the Congregational Church), which

could seat 3,000. Next door was Raper's Temperance Hotel.

And with the chapels the driving force behind the movement, a significant number of teetotal campaigners soon came to focus on one sensitive issue – drinking on Sunday. Petitions proliferated right across Wales to shut pub doors on the Sabbath. Only in cosmopolitan Cardiff was there significant opposition. But there was no stopping the temperance tide, and the Welsh Sunday Closing Act was passed in 1881. It came into effect the following year, just as the Brains took over The Old Brewery.

But, like later Prohibition in the United States, the new law spawned a criminal culture. As the pubs shut, so the shebeens – illegal drinking dens – opened. The police said there were 137 in Temperance Town alone. The ongoing controversy about the effectiveness of the act resulted in a Royal Commission in 1889. S.A. Brain was one of those eager to give evidence.

'The great majority of the private houses in certain districts here have in immense quantities of beer on Saturday nights, and in fact right up to one or two o'clock in the

morning,' he told the Commission. 'It is nothing unusual for the well-conducted licensed victualler to stand at his door on Saturday nights, after he has closed his premises at 11 o'clock, and see brewers' drays and agents' carts delivering 70 or 80 small casks into private houses within 100 yards of his premises.' He stressed that this trade was by outsiders. 'Nearly all the breweries within a radius of 100 miles of Cardiff have sent local agents here.'

He wanted pubs in Cardiff to be allowed to open again on Sunday to end this shady business, which since the Sunday Closing Act came into operation 'has simply deluged the town with illicit drinking'. As a local councillor as well as a brewer, he wanted 'to see the trade properly conducted, so that it will obtain the respect of everyone'.

However, he was to be disappointed. For after touring Wales, the commission found widespread support for the act and simply tightened up its provisions. It was a particularly bitter blow for Brains, since the family had invested heavily in a new brewhouse, as well as buying up pubs.

'PIT OF PROHIBITION'

The teetotallers were triumphant over the Sunday Closing Act. They believed it signalled drink's demise. 'The trumpets are sounding for the Armageddon of Alcohol,' said campaigner Arnold Hills. 'We stand upon the threshold of great events, and as far as the Dominion of Drink is concerned, we are privileged to see the beginning of the end. Already the chains are clanking in the Pit of Prohibition, where the devil of strong drink shall be bound for a full thousand years.'

Brains Brewery, in the distance below, could not avoid the anti-alcohol movement, since dry Temperance Town was built right outside its front door.

The central cellar alone was 300 feet in length and contained 5,000 casks

The sketches from Barnard's book reflect the grand impression made by Brains' new brewhouse.

A Splendid Brewhouse

Though The Old Brewery was the leading brewery in town, it was still a modest affair, just a three-storey stone building behind The Albert pub. The Brains had much bigger ambitions. At first they added another site, by snapping up Watson's Cambrian Brewery in Womanby Street in 1885. But it was when they were able to buy land alongside The Old Brewery that they were really able to expand in 1887.

Alfred Barnard was certainly impressed with the 'splendid brewhouse' they built when he visited a short while later, during research for his book, *Noted Breweries of Great Britain and Ireland*.

'As the visitor enters beneath the archway, he is confronted by the new brewhouse, which is an elegant structure built on the tower principle, with red and white bricks. It is almost fire-proof; iron, brick and concrete forming the principal elements in its construction, whilst its walls are nearly two feet thick. The iron joists which support the massive floors are as broad as a man's body and, with the numerous metal columns (70 in number) which support them, weigh

nearly 50 tons. This brewhouse, which is splendidly arranged, contains a costly and complete plant said to be the largest in South Wales and, together with the new fermenting room, is fitted and ventilated on the most modern principle.'

After meeting S.A. Brain, the visitors were shown around the brewery. Barnard was captivated. 'The mash tun is one of the handsomest we have ever seen, being a fine construction of cast iron encased in varnished pine and bound with massive brass hoops.'

'The copper house adjoining is the prettiest and most complete we have visited.' This was high praise from a man who had inspected most of the leading breweries in Britain. He was dazzled by the 'handsome iron palisading' and 'polished brass rails', while he found the new fermentation department 'a delightful room, lighted by 25 windows'. It contained six 150-barrel fermenting tuns 'constructed of the finest white cedar' each fitted with Clinch's patent attemperators and 'a parachute of new design for carrying off the yeast'.

Below the brewery yard, extensive cellars

had been built, 'floored with vitrified panel bricks' and 'lighted throughout with gas', and connected to the yard above by a platform elevator powered by a six horse-power engine. The central cellar alone was 300 feet in length and contained 5,000 casks.

Brains had not only built a much larger brewhouse, but one with extravagant flourishes. No expense had been spared; it contained the latest equipment. The showpiece plant had cost £50,000.

With such a massive investment, it is no

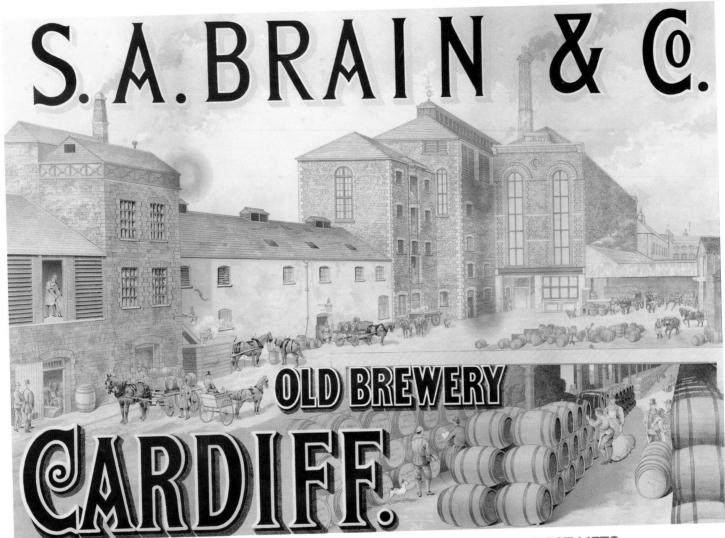

S.A. BRAIN & Co.

OLD BREWERY
CARDIFF.

wonder that S.A. Brain was concerned by the loss of trade on a Sunday, the one day of the week when workers had most spare time on their hands and most money in their pockets. But he had no need to worry, for Cardiff was expanding at such a rapid rate that its population doubled again in 20 years. From 82,700 in 1881 it rocketed to 164,300 by 1901.

His problem was not too little trade, but too much. Even the new brewhouse could not keep up with demand, and he was forced to continue brewing in the old brewhouse as well. Production increased more than 10 times from 100 to 1,100 barrels a week. They had to brew every day of the week – except, of course, on Sunday.

THE LATEST LIFTS

Barnard was shown around using three steam lifts to go up and down the towering building and into the cellars. These platform elevators, made by Thomas and Sons of Cardiff and powered by six horse-power engines, were of the latest design with an automatic stop action.

Mighty Maltings

When Barnard visited Brains' brewhouse, he did not intend to miss another imposing new building in the Victorian boom town. For S.A. Brain in 1886 had been one of the founders of the Cardiff Malting Company in East Moors. Malted barley is the body and soul of good beer and Brains wanted to ensure a reliable supply close to hand.

As Barnard quickly discovered, you could not miss the substantial structure on the harbour skyline. 'Long before we reached our destination, we beheld the extensive maltings belonging to that enterprising company with which Mr Brain's name is associated. They are splendidly situated, being close to the Roath Dock and the railway, therefore convenient for home and seaboard barleys.'

Again little expense had been spared, with local architect F. Baldwin having visited Newark and other major malting centres before drawing up his plans for the mighty mass of malthouses and kilns, 'the finest as well as the largest in The Principality'.

There were two parallel ranges of six-storey maltings, each 172 feet in length, joined together on the top floor above a massive arch running over the company's very own railway siding. There were four germinating floors in each building, a joint barley loft with iron steeping tanks and a series of malt bins in the roof. At the end of each range were two malt kilns, with their distinctive pyramid roofs. Altogether there was storage for 21,600 quarters (one

'The finest as well as the largest in The Principality'

STILL STANDING

The Grade II listed maltings off East Tyndall Street are still a landmark in Cardiff today, but now, instead of being packed with grain, they hold business records, containing more than two million boxes. They are also home to around 20 businesses.

The maltings in the docks were huge structures, where gangs of men, below, worked to turn the malt.

quarter weighed 336lbs) of malt and 8,000 quarters of barley.

Making malt on this large a scale put tremendous strains on the buildings, as the damp grain could be almost a foot deep across floors measuring 112 x 50 feet. The weight and pressure was immense and the thick brick walls and cement floors were supported by heavy iron girders and bulging buttresses.

The malting process is one of the many mysteries of beer. The renowned poet A.E. Houseman declared in *A Shropshire Lad*:

'And malt does more than Milton can
To justify God's way to man.'

For malt is much more than the harvested ears of barley. It involves encouraging the grains to partially germinate by first steeping them in water tanks and then spreading the soaked barley on large germination floors, where it was regularly turned by an army of men to ensure it was well aerated.

The germination turned inaccessible starches in the seeds into sugars, which could later be turned by the brewer into beer. After about five days, the germination was brought to a sharp halt to stop the new sugars being lost, by baking the green malt in kilns for two days at high temperatures. Once the roots are removed, the end product looks little different from the original grain, but the process had transformed the hard seeds into tasty malt, with a crunchy, biscuit texture.

And the malt produced in Cardiff was not only sold to many breweries in South Wales, they also supplied mash tuns as far apart as Burton-upon-Trent and Ireland.

Through these maltings, S.A. Brain intended to have a firmer grasp on Cardiff's frothing glass of beer by controlling its most important raw material.

Brains faced stiff competition for trade in Cardiff from the Burton brewers. An early pub sign for The Old Arcade, right, illustrated the Victorian era. One of its current pubs, The White Hart in James Street, far right, originally sold Allsopp's ales.

TIGHT COMPETITION

The huge number of licensed premises in Victorian Cardiff is best illustrated at the southern end of St Mary Street, where four pubs once stood side by side: The Royal Oak, Blue Anchor, Elliott's Hotel and, on the corner with Mill Lane, The Terminus. Even Brains' grand Golden Cross had another pub in its back pocket. The Fishguard Arms was right next door.

Pub Stampede

When S.A. Brain gave evidence to the Royal Commission on the Welsh Sunday Closing Act in 1889, he was asked a simple question about Brains' public houses in Cardiff, 'Can you state the number?'

'Well, I could not.'

'Not exactly?'

'Well, you see, they are leases; some of them are short and some are long. I could not exactly say the number.'

His reluctance to admit to an exact figure was understandable, for the late Victorian era had seen a huge rush by brewers to snap up pubs and tie their trade after licences were restricted during Gladstone's government of 1869–1874. In this stampede into bricks and mortar, it was often difficult to see a clear picture. S.A. Brain only admitted to owning pubs 'all over the borough and in every division that the police have any superintendence over'.

In 1882, when Brains took over the brewery, only 11 pubs were tied, and only one of these, The Albert, the brewery tap, was included in the purchase. The other 10 were initially retained by John Griffen Thomas, although Brains supplied the beer and had first option to buy them. Within the next two decades, six of the 10 were bought. These included The Golden Cross and The Taff Vale in Queen Street.

Over the same period, Brains worked feverishly to secure other pubs, so that by 1900 the number tied to the brewery had shot up to around 80, with production reaching 1,300 to 1,400 barrels a week. Town guide *Cardiff Up-to-Date* in 1898 said Brains beers 'are supplied to a widespread trade in all parts of Cardiff and the surrounding districts, where the sign boards of the numerous tied houses owned by the firm are familiar local landmarks'.

But Brains was not having the local business all its own way. In the late Victorian era the company faced many local rivals.

In 1885 the town boasted 18 breweries. Major Burton companies like Allsopp's, Ind Coope and Worthington also had agencies in Cardiff, while West Country ventures like Arnold of Wickwar in Gloucestershire and Rogers of Bristol were active in the town, drawn by the booming population.

All these rivals were also seeking to tie up pubs – and there were plenty to target. For the overall total of hotels, inns and public houses in Cardiff had increased considerably, from 27 in 1790 – when the grand jury of the county of Glamorgan thought that the number of alehouses was 'excessive' – to 211 by 1863. Forty years later, in 1903, the figure had reached a staggering 274.

So while Brains had branded its name across 80 pubs, that was less than a third of the total number of licensed premises. But many of them were in the drinking heart of Cardiff – the docks.

By 1900 the number of pubs tied to the brewery had shot up to 80

When the bar shut, the barmaids could sweep up enough coal dust to keep the fires burning

The North & South in Louisa Street, left, was a popular haunt of sailors, while dockers dusted themselves down in The Packet and the West Dock Hotel, right.

Tiger Bay

When S.A. Brain applied to give evidence before the Royal Commission on Sunday Closing in 1889, he stated in his letter of application 'I am the owner of nearly every licensed house in Bute Street, Cardiff.' It was a huge claim, for the long road to the docks from the town centre was peppered with pubs. In 1903 the police recorded 31, plus six off-licences.

But this liquid link road was the heart of Brains' early business. Six of the 11 pubs originally associated with The Old Brewery in 1882 had been on Bute Street, from the Golden Cross at the top to The Crown and Anchor, The Cardigan Arms, The Crown, The Bute Arms and The Prince of Wales. Later additions to the estate included The Glastonbury and The Custom House.

This was Tiger Bay, which once roared with life. A 1927 profile of one pub, The Bute Castle, famous for its boxing ring upstairs, gave a taste of its colourful character. 'There is no inn in Cardiff having more memories of the old sporting days than The Bute Castle down in dockland, with its parrots of all colours and breeds, and its floating cosmopolitan population talking a bewildering number of languages.'

The names of a large number of Brains pubs reflected the salty atmosphere, like The Bosun in Angelina Street and The New Sea Lock in Harrowby Street. At The North & South in Louisa Street, landlady Mrs Bryant acted as an unofficial banker for departing seamen, looking after their valuables while they were at sea. Sailors carried the Brains name around the world as they developed a taste for the beer.

A regular for 40 years at one of the few Brains pubs still standing in Bute Street, The Packet, recalled the days after World War Two. 'Everyone drank Dark or Dark and Bitter mixed. There was no lager in those days. Seamen were used to coming in and trying the local brew. It was a man's pub then, with a big coal fire in winter. Men used to come in off the dock, covered in coal dust, for a pint and a warm-up.'

One of the most familiar landmarks was the solid block of The Mount Stuart opposite the dock gates, which reflected the hard-working prosperity of Cardiff when coal was king. In the palatial back bar, ship owners, sea captains and cargo agents sealed their deals alongside an ornamental bar screen, while the front bar heaved with dusty dockers, coal trimmers and sailors. When this bare bar shut for the afternoon, it was claimed the barmaids could sweep up enough coal dust to keep the fires burning.

You knew the old docks had finally died when this pub closed in 1985, just a short while after a much more imposing Brains house also disappeared a few miles along the coast in another coal port – The Barry Dock Hotel.

CLUB DE MARL

Cardiff Docks also contained the most open act of defiance against the Sunday Closing Act – the Club de Marl. Legendary licensee Bob Downey of The Bute Castle ran this open-air drinking club on a patch of waste ground. Drinkers gathered around a pile of barrels, chucked a few coins onto a sheet and helped themselves to a beer.

Many believed the glasses had to be chained to the solid wooden bar

The Chain Locker

In a bid to break the Marquess of Bute's iron grip on the South Wales coal trade through Cardiff, colliery owner David Davies built a new dock eight miles away at Barry between 1884 and 1889.

It was such an immediate success that Brains saw a golden opportunity to expand its trade beyond Cardiff. Just outside the dock gates, the brewery in 1888 built its grandest licensed premises, The Barry Dock Hotel. It was such a prestigious project that when the company's properties were valued in 1897, it was worth almost as much as the brewery itself – £32,000 compared to the brewery's £40,000. Most pubs were barely worth £1,000.

It was also such a novel venture that a specialist was brought in to run the palatial pile. R.P. Culley already operated The Exchange and The Philharmonic pubs in Cardiff, but the Barry enterprise was on a vastly greater scale. A legend was born.

The imposing structure boasted more than 50 bedrooms, a ballroom, a public hall, commercial rooms, a billiard room, a coffee room and restaurant and 'a splendidly appointed smoke room'. It was twice extended within its first decade.

Special features included a stained-glass window in the reception hall, reflecting colliery winding gear, dark wooden panelling and staircases, carved fireplaces and ornately-plastered ceilings. However, it did not become famous for this grandiose luxury, but rather for the bar down below.

The vaults, which became world renowned, were not entered up the stone stairs to the hotel's pillared main entrance, with its revolving doors, but through a side door off Thompson Street, Barry's lively echo of Cardiff's Bute Street.

Sturdy iron pillars supported a low concrete ceiling. Above was the first-floor cellar from where the beer flowed down to the thirsty sailors, dock workers and navvies alike. The bar

developed such a rowdy reputation that many believed the glasses had to be chained to the solid wooden bar. Hence, it became known as 'The Chain Locker'.

Alexander Cordell captured the unique atmosphere in his novel *Rogues March*. 'More navvies were coming in now, the late shift off the Walnut Tree Viaduct and the great Chain Locker bar was as tight as a barrel of herrings, with men halloing left and right. Big men, most with their clothes in rags, their breeks yorked at the knees with leather or tied with string, grimed and mud-caked, their faces lined with weariness.'

It was a sharp contrast to the plush apartments above, but the bars at The Barry Dock Hotel lasted longer. As the coal trade declined after World War Two, so the hotel's grand rooms fell silent, but The Chain Locker had a longer death rattle. Only in 1982 was the once grand, but decaying building demolished.

But some links to The Chain Locker still live onn. You can find them in Cardiff's Bute Street. The wooden bar-back is now to be found in The Packet, while some of the gas lamps shine again at The Golden Cross.

ON THE WATERFRONT

One survivor of Barry's seafaring past is Brains' imposing Marine pub on Barry Island, where burly dockers also once flexed the anchor tattoos on their arms as they downed pints of Dark. But though the docks and the dockers have long gone, and the premises have been substantially renovated, it is still a pub packed with local character.

The family had not plunged into the often reckless race to go public

Shared Vision

On 23 April 1897, a small report appeared in the *Western Mail*. It began, 'For family reasons, the old-established business of Messrs S.A. Brain & Company has been converted into a limited liability company, with a capital of £400,000.'

It would have been easy to miss this brief mention. Unlike many brewing companies, it was launched without fanfare. There was no blaze of publicity. The reason was simple; it was contained in the report's final sentence. 'There will be no issue of shares to the general public.'

The 12 subscribers were all close family members, the first four being the directors of the company – S.A. Brain, J.B. Brain and his two sons. The others were wives and daughters, plus solicitor W.S. Sweet-Escott, who had married S.A. Brain's daughter, Ethel.

The partners and their nominees retained the whole of the 25,000 preference and 15,000 ordinary £10 shares. The family remained firmly in control. Outsiders were only allowed to buy debenture bonds which 'will be issued to the public as required for further extension of the company's business', said the prospectus. Holders had

no voting rights 'as long as their interest money is regularly paid.'

The firm's name, S.A. Brain & Company, clearly demonstrated who was in charge. S.A. Brain was the first chairman and managing director. But with his banking background, his uncle and partner, Joseph Benjamin Brain, had played a leading role in the limited company's formation. He claimed the first share certificate.

He still lived in Bristol, but significantly both his sons, Joseph Hugh Brain and William Henry Brain, had moved to Cardiff to take a more direct role in the business. They were both described as brewers, like

S.A. Brain. Their father was described as a gentleman of The Mythe, Stoke Bishop.

According to the prospectus, the company's properties were valued at almost £300,000. These included 74 licensed premises made up of 45 fully-licensed pubs, 26 beer houses and three off-licences, almost all in Cardiff. Only three were freehold, the rest being leased. The overall business was valued at £350,000.

The issue of 2,000 £100 debenture bonds to raise a further £200,000 was to pay off existing mortgages and loans, as well as to fund development. The auditors, Price Waterhouse, said profits had risen

CENTENARY CELEBRATIONS

In 1997 the first 100 years of S.A. Brain & Company was marked by the presentation of a Centenary of Incorporation Certificate by John Holden, the registrar of companies for England and Wales. Among those receiving the certificate were the founders' great grandsons, Bill Rhys and Christopher Brain.

from £24,488 in 1894 to £28,533 in 1896. Since then the company had 'acquired several valuable houses'. It added, 'With this extra trade and the saving by additional capital, the vendors believe the profits of the limited company in 1898 will show over £32,000.'

The creation of the registered company reflected both the strength of the business and the careful and conservative nature of the family.

While Brains had spent heavily on a new brewhouse and tying up licensed premises, the family had not plunged into the often reckless race to go public. In creating a limited company, they were a full decade behind local rivals in Cardiff like the Ely Brewery and William Hancock's, which had both registered in 1887.

For while the move to go public offered advantages in raising capital, it also had dangers for the unwary. Even major companies could hit the rocks. Allsopp's of Burton-upon-Trent had been the second-largest brewery in Britain behind Bass, but its headlong rush to buy more and more pubs by issuing more and more shares saw

it come crashing down. By 1911 Allsopp's was in receivership.

Brains were wise to be cautious. And by retaining firm control of the company, the family ensured it remained independent throughout the difficult century ahead.

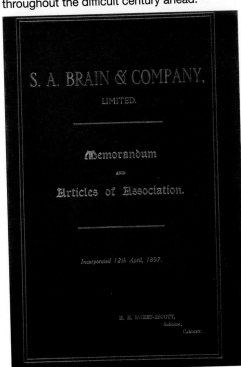

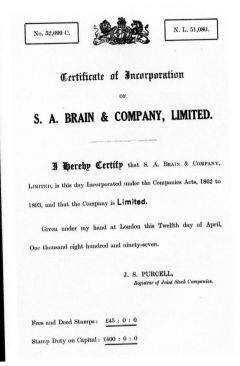

He was active in the politics of Cardiff and became Mayor in 1899

S.A. Brain

S.A. Brain's career mirrored the rise of Cardiff. His stature grew at the same rate as the Victorian boom town. And his life rolled far beyond a barrel of beer.

He had arrived in the expanding borough in 1863, aged only 12 years old. He climbed the brewhouse ladder quickly, eventually running Dowson Brothers' Phoenix Brewery before taking over The Old Brewery with his uncle in 1882 and within five years building a completely new brewhouse, while developing an extensive estate of pubs. In addition, he was one of the founders and the largest shareholder in the Cardiff Malting Company and chairman of South Wales wine merchants Stevens and Sons.

But in the midst of all this frantic industry, he was also highly active in the politics of the port. As the ever-inquisitive Barnard noted in his 1890 book, 'Notwithstanding his manifold duties in the brewery, Mr S.A. Brain finds time to interest himself in the affairs of the town, and is one of the most popular members of the county council, having been elected to that office in 1885.

'He is also on most of the important committees, such as finance, health and

His military rank gave S.A. Brain added status when he became Mayor of Cardiff in 1899, for his term of office coincided with the tensions of the Boer War, in which many Welsh soldiers were involved. When the news was announced on 17 May 1900 that the beseiged town of Mafeking had been relieved after 207 days, people poured on to the streets of Cardiff to celebrate – and, as Mayor, he toured the town in an open landau.

'St Mary Street presented a wonderful sight. Excited crowds paraded, singing, shouting, cheering, yelling, roaring with delirious glee. Bells – from the small table bells to the porters' big ear-splitting instruments – were ringing out,' reported the *South Wales Daily News*. Elsewhere there were fireworks and bonfires – and many pints of Brains were drunk.

It was a colourful finale to a remarkable career, for within three years he had died, aged only 52.

sanitary boards, and is a member of nearly every friendly society in the town.'

Since many of the friendly societies, which helped working men in times of need, met in pubs, it was a shrewd move to develop close links with them. But S.A. Brain genuinely enjoyed their company. As he told the Royal Commission on Welsh Sunday Closing in 1889, 'I mix a great deal with the public and with the working classes and I am very proud of the working classes. I have always found them very straightforward men.'

As the councillor for the working-class ward of Grangetown in Cardiff, he saw himself as a practical man of the people. He was described in 1893, in a commercial profile of the ports of the Bristol Channel, as 'one of the most popular and energetic members of Cardiff County Council'.

The commercial profile of the brewery spent as much time praising the man as describing his business. He seemed as towering as his new brewhouse. It concluded, 'His unfailing interest in the welfare of the working classes in the town, coupled with his active participation in every public movement having a beneficial object, has won for him the esteem and regard of all sections of society.'

His political opponents might disagree, but he was popular. That same year he was returned with a large majority at the head of the poll for the Cardiff School Board.

He was also a captain in the local artillery volunteers. Cartoonists, right, delighted in depicting him as a military man in his political battles on the council.

Put Up To Be Knocked Down.

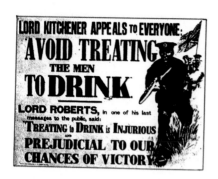

'Drink is doing us more damage in the war than all the German submarines put together'

Fighting for Survival

Following S.A. Brain's death in 1903, what followed was the calm of consolidation in the new city (Cardiff gained city status in 1905). His uncle and co-founder Joseph Benjamin Brain took over as chairman for four years followed by Joseph's two sons, the well-known Glamorgan cricketers, J.H. Brain (1907–14) and W.H. Brain (1914–34).

But while Brains was now an established and prominent part of the city, the brewing industry was not so secure. In fact, as the war clouds gathered over Europe in 1914, it faced a battle for survival.

'Drink is doing us more damage in the war than all the German submarines put together,' thundered Minister of Munitions David Lloyd George in 1915. 'We are fighting Germany, Austria and drink; and as far as I can see the greatest of these three deadly foes is drink.'

The fiery Welsh politician, who was to become Prime Minister in 1916, was one of two avowed teetotallers in the five-man war cabinet. He had supported complete prohibition in Wales since the 1880s, but bills to introduce such measures had been repeatedly blocked in the House of Commons by what Lloyd George described as 'the brewers' ring which seems

to govern England'. Now, under the cloak of the national emergency, he was determined to gain his revenge.

This war within a war had already claimed a number of casualties. First to be shot down was all-day drinking in vital areas. As a strategic port, Cardiff was soon snared. New orders in 1915 restricted weekday pub opening times to just five-and-a-half hours a day, from 12-2.30pm at lunchtime and 6-9pm in the evening. On Saturday it was worse. Landlords had to call time an hour earlier at 8pm. Even 'treating' or buying in rounds was prohibited. Brains new chairman, W.H. Brain, who was also president of the South Wales Brewers' Association, described the changes 'as a great blow to the trade'.

It was not the only blow though. The brewing industry had to shoulder a huge burden of wartime taxation, doubling the cost of the cheapest pint from 2d to 4d between 1914 and 1916. It also had to struggle against a severe shortage of men and materials and restrictions on output, which almost halved production from over 37 million barrels in 1913 to 19 million in 1917. The average strength of beer collapsed to below 3 per cent alcohol. In some areas, like

Not in the Peace Treaty—
Still Your Enemy

Carlisle, brewing companies and pubs were taken over by the government, with many closed down.

The industry was on its knees and facing oblivion. The United States was moving towards total prohibition and expected its ally to follow. Food administrator Herbert Hoover issued veiled threats that an increase in American grain exports would be difficult to secure without an end to brewing in Britain. Lloyd George was eager to oblige. Temperance leaders urged action 'while the overshadowing issues of war are accustoming the people to restricted liberties'.

It was against this bleak background that Brains issued a defiant notice in the local *Evening Express* on Saturday, 15 July 1916: 'We believe there is to be an effort made by a few busybodies with time on their hands, who take advantage of the absence of the brave fellows who are fighting so nobly for us and for them, to promote the cause (if it be a cause) of prohibition: that is, they have the effrontery to suggest, because they have neither the head nor the stomach to appreciate good beer, therefore all men and women must be compelled to drink water.

TRAGIC LOSS

The brewery not only suffered the hardship of war in the difficult trading conditions, but also the threat of prohibition and the loss of many employees. Brains also felt the pain much closer to home – in their own family. William Arthur Sweet-Escott, the eldest son of S.A. Brain's daughter, Ethel, was killed in action in 1918.

Lloyd George, below, was determined to ride over the brewing industry in his drive to war. Even in victory, left, temperance campaigners reminded soldiers that booze was still the enemy.

FIGHTING FOR SURVIVAL

EMPTY BARS

The harsh licensing restrictions came as a shock to both landlords and pub customers. But some, at first, still opened at their usual times, in the hope of compensation. One Cardiff licensee recalled the first morning:

'The door was opened at 5.30am with a "business as usual" spirit … The mullers, bright and shining, are filled and ready with good, piping-hot tea and coffee. In full view of any customer that may enter is a display of Bovril and biscuits. All is ready to supply anything in the refreshment business – excepting intoxicants.

'Just five minutes to six, one of the sons of toil enters and asks for a rum. The request is met with the answer, "Sorry, sir, but you cannot have a rum. Will a coffee or tea suit?". "Coffee or tea! Strewth! I want something to stay my stomach with … I have no time to stay over long hot drinks – must get on the job".'

And he was gone – like most other customers. One bar with a staff of five reported selling just a packet of cigarettes in the morning. It was to be a long, hard war.

'The suggestion is an insult to a hard-working, law-abiding, sober country, which has other matters on hand just now than answering silly questions of intemperate people who lack good taste as well as good manners. The British Empire – which they are oh so proud of – was not built by water drinkers and conscientious objectors.

'There is no question that men and women should have the opportunity for practising and showing self-control amidst the opportunities for over indulgence – in that lies virtue. The drinking of beer is a wholesome habit practised by the British nation (in fact by all virile people, bishops and laymen alike) for many generations, and in the year 1916 conscientious objectors are not found among beer drinkers.'

Brains felt confident in making this statement, since one of their pubs, the Neptune Inn, above, alongside the brewery in Caroline Street, was one of the leading recruitment centres for the army in Cardiff. Under the patriotic landlord, Mr S. Reed, the walls of the pub were plastered with posters promoting the Welsh Guards and urging

"Up Guards And At 'Em."

— By A SPECIAL REPORTER.

PARROT'S CRY in a CARDIFF INN which has been the

Recruiting Centre For Seven Wars.

IN a house in Cardiff that has been a recruiting centre for seven wars I heard to-day stories of the past, was shown relics of stirring days, of old-time battles, and listened to a very modern parrot shouting, " Echo, Two o'clock winner," and " Up, Guards, and at 'em."

The house is the Neptune Inn, Caroline-street, and while the landlord, Mr. Samuel Reed, who at 79 years of age must be one of the oldest barmen in Wales, was regaling me with tales of the Zulu War, the African War, and his experiences as an unofficial recruiting officer, the parrot kept up his raucous squawking as though to emphasise the contrast of age and modernity.

I had entered the Neptune Inn through a narrow, old-fashioned passage-way.

On the left-hand side was the door to a tiny bar, but in that tiny bar were many military relics of a hundred years ago, recruiting pictures, yellow and cracked with age, and the very Bible and Testament upon which soldiers swore allegiance on the field of battle their allegiance to their Sovereign and country.

Fighting for King and Queen.

The Neptune Inn has been in the ownership of the same family since 1848. It has been the scene of countless occasions when resplendently-equipped recruiting officers have fired the imagination of Cardiff men with thrilling stories of the glories of fighting for Queen and King.

The next moment the thrilled civilian would feel the King's shilling pressed into his palm.

A few days later he was a soldier or sailor.

"That," said Mr Reed, or Sam, as he prefers to be called, " was how it was done.

" During the Great War alone my rifle and I recruited 4,500 men in this house."

Sam claims—rightly, it seems—that he is the oldest landlord and barman in Wales, and that the Neptune Inn is the oldest military and naval rendezvous in the country.

" My wife's father owned the hotel before us," he said, " and I was brought up here when I was a baby in arms. I have remained here ever since. Men have been recruited here for the Army and Navy for the Ashanti War, the Boer War, the Indian Mutiny, the Zulu War, the Peninsula War and the Great War.

From the bar there is another short length of passage leading to an old-fashioned, stone-floored smokeroom. The walls are of solid stone, and the plain, aged ornaments plentifully interspersed with almost obliterated posters illustrating the honour of being a fighting man.

Those self-same posters many years ago played their parts in persuading men to take the oath of allegiance.

Through another door there is the old paved passage-way along which the men would walk to be measured and weighed.

THE HISTORIC NEPTUNE INN.

And standing covered in dust in a gloomy corner is the identical height-testing appliance.

Upon its broad footstand are the indentations made by thousands of feet —feet of men who one day were drinking in the tiny bar, and the next were en route to be trained to fight for their country.

Mr. Sam Reed himself is an old soldier. He joined the 24th Cumberland Regiment just after the Indian Mutiny—and he takes pride in recalling the fact that he, too, was recruited in the Neptune Inn.

His reminiscences of the excitement of old-time war days are as stirring as they are interesting.

" I have seen boys and men come in ting 70 or 80 men they said they still needed another three or four.

" After they had gone I noticed a shoe-black standing in the street and asked him if he would like to join up. He was backward at first, but I finally persuaded him. He asked me what we should do with his boot-box and blacking brushes, and I told him I would look after them.

" And I did," said Sam. " He joined up and I haven't seen him from that day to this—but his boot-box is still here, waiting for him to claim it."

Mrs Reed, too, has been of great assistance to Sam in his recruiting efforts. She is 66, and to-day sleeps in the same bed in which she was born.

" The first Guards Regiment was formed in 1815," said Mrs Reed, " and my father recruited for it in this very room 115 years ago."

While Mrs Reed was speaking there occurred a remarkable coincidence. Into the room walked a man who joined up in the bar of the Neptune 40 years ago.

Sam welcomed him warmly, and then went on to speak of the pride and pleasure he always took in persuading men to fight for their King and country.

" Ever since I can remember," he said, " I have always felt elated when, through my own efforts, I have recruited men for the British Army or Navy."

... the European War Sam was a very brave man. The welfare of his little hotel was a secondary consideration to the task of swelling the ranks of the Allied forces.

Hundred after hundred men he recruited in his tap-room, took their names, and packed them off to the barracks to be enlisted.

" I was too old to fight myself," he said, " but I could at least use what influence I had to persuade younger men that their duty was at the front."

Chip off the Old Block.

Sam is a chip off the old block. Different men have different hobbies. His hobby has been the "collecting" of fighting men.

" But," he concluded, " all the wars I have experienced have taught me that while recruiting is well enough, war itself is a terrible tragedy. Many men go out, but few come back."

And as the reporter walked out into Caroline-street he heard the cynical voice of the parrot: " This is the place. Army or Navy. Echo: Two o'clock winner. Up, Guards, and—"

—J.M.

Mr and Mrs SAM REED,

here for a drink," he told the reporter, " who looked narrow-chested and unhealthy. They were spoken to by the recruiting officers. They joined the services, and a few months later they again came into the Neptune, but then I hardly knew them. Military and naval training had made new men of them.

The Shoe-black who never came.

" I remember one occasion at the commencement of the last war when a couple of recruiting officers came in here. They wanted recruits for the Monmouthshire Militia and after get-

---

young men 'to do their duty'. One notice alongside the bar entrance proclaimed 'This way to the Front!'

Another newspaper notice concluded, 'We suggest that men and women should decide for themselves whether they will drink ale or not, and not allow this peculiar section of the community to decide what other people shall do. For anyone to say "I don't want a glass of ale, therefore YOU shall not have one" is nothing less than priggish insolence.

'Our fighting men and our working men and women have the liberty – and mean to preserve it – to decide whether they will drink water or merely wash in it. May we ask the clear-thinking and broad-minded folk of Cardiff to give a decided "NO" if they are asked to sign any petition which suggests that the sale of beer, wines and spirits should be prohibited entirely because they are intoxicating when over-indulged in. Say "NO" then carefully shut the door.'

W.H. Brain would probably have much preferred them to slam it. This tirade shows how much pressure Brains was under. The whole future of the business was in severe danger. But the company was right to make this remarkable public appeal, for in the end it was public pressure which prevented prohibition.

In March 1917, Britain's food controller, Lord Devonport, moved to further limit brewing to just 28 per cent of its pre-war level, a mere 10 million barrels. This target was never reached, because of swelling public anger. The Home Secretary, Sir George Cave, told the Commons in July, 'The beer shortage is causing considerable unrest, and is interfering with the output of munitions and with the position of the country in this war. There is discontent, loss of time, loss of work and in some cases even strikes are threatened and indeed caused by the shortage of beer.'

Restrictions were relaxed and output rose to 23 million barrels in 1918. Brains had survived its darkest hour.

'The British Empire was not built by water drinkers and conscientious objectors'

The New Brewery

The war also left its scars on the company's major development of the troubled and challenging era – a completely new brewery in the Cardiff suburbs at Roath.

The Old Brewery had been struggling to keep up with the demand for Brains beers before the conflict, particularly in the growing market for bottled beer, and so the board decided to build an additional plant away from the cramped city centre site.

In the late 1890s it had already established a bottling store in Nora Street in Roath. Then, a larger site between Nora Street and Helen Street was bought, and work began on building a new brewhouse. The red brick tower was topped out in 1914, just as the war began – which meant the first brew was not put through until a full five years later, as the company's expansion was put on hold during the long national emergency.

The austere building which finally emerged was in sharp contrast to the rebuilt Old Brewery, which had so entranced Barnard in 1890. There was no 'handsome iron palisading' or 'polished brass rails' this time, just a functional plant to rattle out crates of bottled beer, leaving The Old Brewery to roll out barrels of traditional draught ales. At the same time, the original three-storey brewery behind The Albert was demolished in 1919.

As well as standard pints and half-pint

WET AND DRY

The siting of The New Brewery was a red rag to a raging bull for the temperance movement, as it was built next door to Diamond Street United Methodist Chapel which had been established with the help of the leading Cardiff temperance campaigners and ship owners, the Cory family.

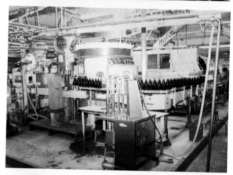

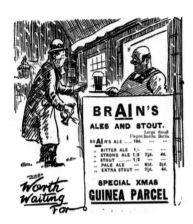

Flagons were the Sunday sustainers, sold at very reasonable prices

bottles, The New Brewery also produced larger two-pint flagons, which were in great demand in Wales to help see thirsty customers through the dry Sabbath. A wide range of beers were sold in these heavyweight containers, including Brains ale, mild, bitter, strong ale and stout. Before canned beer and six-packs, these were the Sunday sustainers, sold at very reasonable prices. The ale and mild in flagons cost just 10d for two pints in 1934, compared to 6d a pint for draught Red Dragon (Dark) in a pub.

The flagons were also the subject of an old Cardiff joke down the decades. A football fan at a Cardiff City versus Swansea derby match at Ninian Park consoles his neighbour, as the big glass bottles fly over their heads. 'Don't worry. You know what they say. It won't hit you, if it hasn't got your name on it.' The other man ducks. 'That's the trouble. I'm Mr Brain.'

Besides bottling Brains' own beers, The New Brewery also bottled the brews of other companies which were sold in Brains houses like Guinness or Bulmer's cider. One part of the brewery was still known as the Bass cellar, long after Brains stopped selling bottled, red-label Bass from Burton-upon-Trent.

In 1932 Brains also began to make and bottle their own soft drinks at The New Brewery under the Spa Table Waters label. These included ginger beer, lemonade, tonic water, cola and bitter lemon, as well as soda water in siphons.

This new development would have pleased the temperance campaigners, but their influence was beginning to sharply decline.

A Brains off-licence in Wellington Street, Canton, promotes the brewery's flagons.
Below: Advertising from the 1920's.

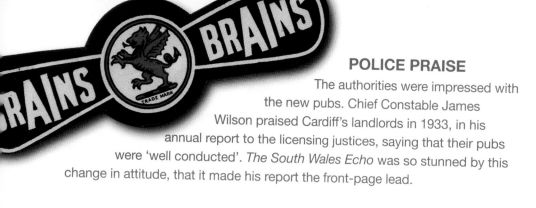

POLICE PRAISE
The authorities were impressed with the new pubs. Chief Constable James Wilson praised Cardiff's landlords in 1933, in his annual report to the licensing justices, saying that their pubs were 'well conducted'. *The South Wales Echo* was so stunned by this change in attitude, that it made his report the front-page lead.

Pubs fit for Heroes

When World War One ended, the brewing industry was left licking its wounds. It had been given a great fright, having come close to being closed down. It was not so much the wartime restrictions – these were to be expected in a national emergency – it was the openly hostile atmosphere. The government were of the belief that the brewers were in the opposite trenches along with the enemy.

With prohibition having been fully adopted in the United States in 1920, the temperance movement was rampant. After all, what America does today, the UK usually does tomorrow. The industry needed to build bridges fast with the authorities. It also needed to build a better reputation on the streets. And the best way to do this was to build and run better pubs.

'Fifty years ago [in 1879] the generality of public houses, especially in the towns, stood on a rather low level. The bad type of house was deplorable, with its dingy taproom, ill-kept floor, sloppy counter and stale atmosphere. The parlours and saloons of the houses just above this class were, as a rule, either ill-kept or gaudy. The flaring

lights and staring mirrors of the gin palace were as objectionable as the murk and gloom of the den.'

This was not the biased view of an ardent teetotaller, but an honest assessment by one of Britain's leading brewers, Mitchells & Butlers of Birmingham in 1929. The company could well afford to take this disparaging look at its past because it was one of the leading advocates of 'improved public houses', a movement which had been triggered by the guns of World War One.

When the government had nationalised the brewing industry in the Carlisle area in 1916, because it was concerned about drunkenness affecting munitions production, the state management had then closed many pubs and replaced them with 'model houses', with more emphasis on food, better facilities for women, games and entertainment. Comfortable seating was intended to end 'vertical drinking'. Some brewers were impressed by this policy of 'fewer but better pubs' – including Brains.

The company in 1929 replaced the stark Birchgrove on Caerphilly Road, with its huge

The Birchgrove looked as if it ought to be approached down a long tree-lined drive

painted wall signs proclaiming 'It's BrAIns You Want', right, with a building which is more a country mansion than a pub, with towering chimneys and an elaborate roof, above. It looks as if it ought to be approached down a long, tree-lined drive, rather than off a busy main road.

But no-one should have been surprised, for it was designed by leading architect Sir Percy Thomas, who was responsible for some of Wales' landmark buildings including Swansea Guildhall. He enjoyed the architecture of pubs so much, he also redesigned another prominent Brains house, the Westgate Hotel, left, in the early 1930s, and his firm was later the hand behind two completely new Brains houses in Cardiff – The Culverhouse and The Three Arches.

At the same time, many smaller houses were closed. The number of pubs in the city fell by almost a quarter in the 30 years after 1903, down 69 to around 200.

HOME BREWED

Brains' flagship beer between the wars was Home Brewed, a strong double brown ale which was only sold in nip-size bottles and half-pints, but not in pints or flagons. At 5d a half in 1934 it was Brains' most expensive bottled brew alongside IPA. But its rich taste was not to survive the privations of the next global conflict.

Beer is Best

The wartime restrictions had not ceased with the end of the war. Many were continued in the 1921 Licensing Act, notably the limitations on pub hours. Bars continued to close for most of the morning and in the afternoon, with last orders at night at 10.30pm or earlier. There was no return to all-day drinking.

At the same time the heavy burden of wartime taxation was barely lifted. This ensured prices never reverted to their pre-war level – and more significantly, ale never regained its pre-war strength. Some of the strongest brews, notably Brains 'Little Imp'

or Imperial Stout, vanished altogether. They were casualties of war.

These factors meant that the drunk, a familiar feature of Victorian and Edwardian Cardiff, staggered off the streets. From a peak of 1,667 cases in 1897, the number had plunged to just 158 by 1932. Cardiff had almost slid off the legless table. This was a major transformation and the new sober spirit of the age saw support for the hard-line temperance movement begin to drain away.

Attempts to introduce prohibition were also undermined by the alarming experience

in the United States, where a whole new criminal culture had thrived on the demand for illicit booze. Instead of portraying a mighty moral nation, the new US image was one of gangsters and guns. Al Capone had replaced upright Uncle Sam. By the end of 1933 the discredited law had been repealed.

Many Cardiff residents were not at all impressed when the teetotal Alderman C.F. Sanders became Lord Mayor in 1932 and declared it would be a 'dry civic year' with no alcohol at receptions, including the Lord Mayor's Banquet at the City Hall.

When the dry event took place, *South*

CARTOON BY J. C. WALKER

TO-DAY'S REHEARSAL OF THE LORD MAYOR'S SHOW

The Lord Mayor's Banquet, which takes place at the City Hall (Cardiff) to-morrow, will be "dry."

The campaign helped to restore the standing of beer as the national drink

I drink beer
BECAUSE
It does me good
I like it
beer is best

Wales Echo cartoonist, J.C. Walker, depicted the brewers as mourners at a funeral, following the Lord Mayor's 'hearse' carrying a 'dead' barrel of beer, left. A camel humped in mineral waters instead. Opponents claimed the council had lost thousands of pounds since the drinks ban – and drinkers were sneaking in bottles anyway. The tide was turning.

The brewers could afford to smile. Official hostility was vanishing, and with their improved pubs, the industry was becoming respectable. The trade had come in from the cold. There was just one major problem. In this new climate, there was a lot less beer being drunk than in the past.

And when the depression began to bite in the early 1930s, this became a serious issue. As unemployment spread, drinkers had little in their pockets apart from their idle hands. Beer sales crashed to the lowest point of the century, dropping to below 18 million barrels in 1932 – less than half the annual production in 1900.

In response, the industry in 1933 launched a 'Beer is Best' poster and advertising campaign across the country. Brains backed this huge co-operative venture – and it worked. Production rose to more than 25 million barrels by 1939. It also helped to restore the standing of beer as the national drink, led by the continuing switch to bottled beer.

Brains bought a steam wagon in 1907 and within 10 years owned six

Fresh Horsepower

In the 1896 guide *Cardiff: An Illustrated Handbook*, S.A. Brain demonstrated just how vital horses were in the running of a Victorian brewery. Without them, the heavy barrels of beer could never be delivered, and so they were looked after in some style. The brewery chairman described their accommodation at length.

'The firm is very well known for its excellent horses, and the animals receive every attention and care. The stables, which are model establishments, stand at the back of the building, and consist of one long range, comprising 10 stalls and several boxes. Overhead are hay, corn and fodder lofts, fitted with engines and other machinery for crushing corn and chaff cutting. There is a horse-washing yard close by, supplied with hot and cold water, and a harness room.'

Barnard had been impressed when in 1890 he visited the 'new model stables' at the Llanelli brewery of Buckleys, which Brains was later to take over. 'All the brewery horses are grey, so also are the hunters and carriage horses belonging to the partners. This splendid stud of 18 horses, which has no equal in Wales, was selected by William Buckley, who is said to be one of the best judges of horseflesh in The Principality. Most of the horses were out, but among those resting for the day we recognised a shire-bred and a Yorkshire grey, the latter a magnificent animal.'

These horses did not just provide the horsepower to deliver the beer; these graceful creatures, striding through the streets, were one of the best ways to promote the brewery. They had just one drawback. They could only supply a limited area around the brewhouse. Ambitious firms, seeking to expand their trade, needed more horse power. And they found it in the new steam wagons. Breweries were among the first companies to embrace these strange, smoking beasts.

Brains bought a Yorkshire steam wagon in 1907 and within 10 years owned six steamers, including two Thorneycrofts. But

Dray horses at the Crown Brewery, Pontyclun, below, and at Buckley's Brewery in Llanelli, above, but Brains was quick to put its faith in steam wagons, right.

these mechanical monsters could be difficult to drive. They needed two men to operate them – a driver whose view was obscured by a central vertical chimney and a steerer using a wheel at the side.

Fred Jarvis, who joined Brains in 1917, remembers them well. 'They did eight mph. They were coal-powered. The driver was inside by the boiler stoking up and his mate sat outside in all winds and weathers doing the steering with a great big wheel.' With their suspect braking and solid metal

wheels, they were not easy to control despite the slow speeds.

Many draymen still preferred genuine 'horse' power and not just because the animals were easier to handle. They could also steer themselves. 'I remember one old fellow, Tom Warren. He did local deliveries and he'd get a pint in every pub,' said Fred Jarvis. 'At the end of the day he'd be snoozing in his seat and the horses would bring him back to the yard.'

There was great loyalty to Brains among the workers. Some stayed all their working lives. Fred Jarvis retired in 1971 as chief engineer. The loyalty was reciprocated by the management. Fred remembers seeing one of the bosses holding a dozy drayman's head under a gushing cold water tap in the yard to sober him up rather than sack him.

One or two steamers survived until World War Two, but by then more conventional petrol-driven lorries had taken over most deliveries.

SMASHING OFFER

One Brains steam wagon going up Warren Hill in Barry once slipped back – right into a pawnshop. The driver kept his head, leaped out and asked the distraught pawnbroker, gazing in amazement at the vehicle in his shop, 'How much for this lot?'.

'The pub brings people together in a spirit of comradeship and cements the common purpose'

Call for –
DRAUGHT BEER
AND HELP YOUR COUNTRY BY SAVING –
GLASS
RUBBER
TIMBER
PETROL
LABOUR

Draught Beer is good

Blockhouse on the Home Front

When war clouds gathered again in 1939, the brewing industry was facing a very different battle from 25 years before.

The temperance movement's renewed call for severe restrictions was this time roundly rejected. Oxford MP Quintin Hogg bluntly told his local dry lobby, 'The national emergency is not a moment to introduce temperance propaganda under the cloak of national necessity. Beer is the innocent pleasure among many millions, especially among those who bear the brunt today.'

The hard work between the wars in making the trade respectable had paid off. Instead of being seen as the enemy behind the lines, the government viewed both beer and the pub as vital for maintaining morale at home. But that did not mean there were no problems ahead.

After the early 'phoney war', when the main concerns for Brains were the commandeering of their better vehicles and the call up of some workers, plus a rise in beer duty, the conflict began to bite once Hitler swept into France. As a prominent port, Cardiff was suddenly in the frontline. Bombs began to hit home, damaging

famous pubs like The Custom House on Bute Street, below.

Gradually all the raw materials of the business started to dry up, from bottles and stoppers to staff, besides fuel for the remaining lorries. Customers were urged to

'*Remember men, if you want the beer to last out for the week, make every shot count*'

LIGHTS OUT

Mrs Florence Deeley, landlady of The Duke of Wellington in The Hayes, close to Brains brewery, fell foul of the wartime restrictions soon after the conflict began. On Friday 13 October 1939 it was reported by police that 'during the hours of darkness, she did cause a light to be displayed in the pub without it being obscured to prevent any illumination being visible from outside.' She was given a warning.

switch to draught beer to save on glass, rubber, timber (for crates), petrol and labour. Even pub glasses were in short supply – and it wasn't the fault of the enemy.

'Stolen from Tom Dancer' was the inscription the landlord of The British Volunteer in The Hayes had sandblasted on his glasses in World War One. 'We are experiencing a repetition of stealing on the same scale as then,' a Cardiff publican told the *Daily Herald*. 'Glasses are becoming so scarce that we may have to use jam jars, as we did during the last war.'

Sacks of malt and hops were also running low, so the strength of beer was slashed to eke out supplies. But it did not reduce demand. Pubs regularly ran out of beer.

Thirsty customers started to panic buy, fearing their next pint could be their last. Draymen from the United Clubs Brewery of Pontyclun recall delivering a barrel of beer to a Valleys club which had run dry, and by the time they had finished their complimentary glass at the bar, members had drained the cask.

The pub was taking on a central role in the conflict, becoming 'a thing of far greater significance than it has ever been', reported Rupert Croft-Cooke on a tour of the country. 'It brings people together in a spirit of companionship and cements the common purpose. The inn is a blockhouse on the home front.'

Pubs and clubs also raised huge amounts for the war effort, and not just through the increased duty on beer. Almost every bar set up savings stamps groups to support events like Warships Week or the 'Tank'ard Fund. Posters were stuck on pub walls showing a cowering Hitler with the slogan 'Stamp on the Blighter'.

Teetotallers were impressed. 'Aquarius' wrote to the *Western Mail*, admitting that drinkers 'are shouldering a very heavy proportion of the financial burden imposed by the war'. He called on fellow abstainers to contribute £1 to the Spitfire Fund.

Even the temperance movement was drinking in the co-operative spirit of the conflict. Old foes were united against a common enemy.

A fighter plane is loaded on to a ship in Cardiff docks.

After the adrenalin rush of the war, the country was exhausted

The Pint in Peace

World War Two had finally settled two scores – Hitler and the temperance movement. 'The war has broken up many old prejudices and dispelled many deep-rooted illusions. None, perhaps, has been more completely shattered than the idea that the devil lurks at the bottom of every glass of beer,' predicted the Brewing Trade Review as early as May 1943.

However, there was one threat still lurking in the wings – nationalisation. A radical Labour Government had been elected in 1945. One of its leading figures, Herbert Morrison, while Home Secretary in the War Cabinet, had visited Carlisle in 1941. He had sampled the state beer, played bowls at one of the state pubs and been impressed. When asked about extending state control, he had replied, 'The scheme has been eminently successful, and the moral is pretty clear.'

Now Labour was in power, many brewers had begun to sweat over their beer glasses. Nationalisation was embracing everything from the coal mines and steel to the railways. Would breweries be next? The industry's protection lay in the high regard

in which the pub was now held. There was very little public pressure for a change of ownership at a time when Labour was wrestling with more pressing issues like establishing the NHS. The danger passed.

Instead, breweries faced a more grim reality. After the adrenalin rush of the war, the country was exhausted. Britain slumped back to the depressed years of the 1930s. Rationing ruled and investing in worn-out plant and run-down pubs was sharply restricted. After the feverish thirst of 1945, when UK beer production had topped 32.6 million barrels, annual post-war demand bumped along below 25 million until the late 1950s.

Brains faced another problem. 'There was a shortage of family in the business after the war, so six weeks after I was demobbed in 1946, I joined the company,' said S.A. Brain's great-grandson Bill Rhys. There was no comfortable desk job waiting for him. Instead he started work as a brewer. 'That involved getting up at 6am to get the brew going, then following it through till it was collected between 4 and 5pm.'

In the meantime, the former company

Trade was far from brisk at The Albert when Bill Rhys, top, joined the brewery in 1946.

secretary George Walters was chairman, the only non-family member to lead the firm, from 1941 to 1952. He was briefly followed by the return of one of Bill Rhys' older relatives, Horace Hay Sweet-Escott, who had been chairman before the war until Joseph Brain's grandson, Michael Brain, took over in 1955. It was an auspicious moment, for Brains was about to make its first significant expansion after the war.

Early in 1956 the brewery bought five prominent Cardiff pubs belonging to local wine merchants Greenwood & Brown for around £100,000. These were The Model Inn in Quay Street, described at the time as 'one of the best-known chop-houses' in the capital, above, plus The York Hotel on Canal Wharf, The Vulcan in Adam Street, The Ship Hotel in Cardiff Docks and The Cross Inn at Rumney.

It was a solid statement of confidence in the future at a time when many family breweries were becoming disillusioned by poor trade in the face of increasing competition from the new threat to the pub – television.

KEEN SPORTSMAN

Michael Benjamin Brain was to be one of Brains' longest-serving chairmen, keeping the company independent through the difficult decade of the 1960s when many family breweries were taken over by the new national breweries, until his death in 1971 at the age of 61. Like his father, he was also a keen sportsman. His main interest was shooting, but he was also a cricket and rugby enthusiast.

The Old Arcade is as famous to rugby fans around the world as Cardiff Arms Park

"THERE MUST BE SUMMAT GOOD ON TELLY TONIGHT"

Licensed Legends

As television flickered into life some believed that the 'goggle box' could call time on the long-term future of the pub. Brains' local rival, the Ely Brewery, even produced a bottled TV Ale in flagons in a desperate bid to capture some of the expected stay-at-home market.

But the fears ignored the powerful ingrained habit of popping down the pub. Many pubs were the social centres of life in their local community, providing the headquarters for everything from local rugby, baseball and cricket teams to cycling, pigeon and rambling clubs. They also offered their own bar sports, from darts and dominoes to billiards and the Cardiff speciality of skittles – many boasting their own alley.

Brains houses in Cardiff were licensed legends in their own streets – and sometimes far beyond. The Old Arcade in Church Street is as familiar to rugby fans around the world as Cardiff Arms Park and The Millennium Stadium, while many rugby internationals, such as 'Wick' Powell and his brother Jack, became popular licensees, drawing in drinkers.

Other Brains pubs are recorded in literature. The Insole Arms in Harvey Street, Canton, was described in writer Howard Spring's colourful autobiography, *Heaven Lies About Us*, recalling his childhood in Cardiff, when he hung around the enticing brass-barred door of the corner pub. Like many, it was better known by the name of the landlord.

'Joe Andrew's public house stood at the intersection of the roads; and in a corner of the wall was the tar-blackened buttress that was Joe Andrew's Stone. The fathers of the street met in Joe Andrew's bright bar; the boys consorted each night at the Stone. For us the Stone was a landmark as geographically important as the Cape or the Horn to more distant wanderers.'

Kitty Flynn in the boxing ring at The Royal Oak holding Jim Driscoll's Lonsdale belt.

Pubs are always landmarks, though some stand out more than others. Brains' striking Wyndham Hotel, left, used to confront travellers as they headed west out of Cardiff on the Cowbridge Road, sharply dividing the A4055 to Barry from the A48 to Port Talbot.

But it is the characters surrounding the bars who are best remembered. And none left a longer trail around Cardiff's pubs than ring legend 'Peerless' Jim Driscoll. He was not only one of Wales' best boxers, a European featherweight champion, but he also linked up pubs across the capital, having run one in Newtown, trained in others in the docks and been long revered in a third across town.

He was born in Ellen Street, Newtown, in 1880 and died little more than 44 years later, just a few doors away in The Duke of Edinburgh, where he was the landlord. During his short life his reputation had soared out of the humble street, and after his death and the closure of The Duke his memory was kept alive in The Royal Oak in Roath, which has its own boxing ring. The pub was run by Jim's relatives, including Welsh rugby international Jim 'Ocker' Burns and then his daughter Kitty Flynn until 2003, and it was packed full of his boxing mementoes. The Cambrian pub on the corner of St Mary Street and Caroline Street was recently renamed 'Kitty Flynn's' in her memory.

It was a place you had to visit – like many other Brains houses.

PINT AND THE PULPIT

One Brains house, The Lewis Arms in Tongwynlais, was used by the famous preacher Christmas Evans in 1827 to deliver a sermon for the Welsh Baptists. This was shortly before the pint and the pulpit became sworn enemies, with the rise of the temperance movement in the nonconformist chapels. A plaque in the pub commemorates the event.

LICENSED LEGENDS

Snuff boxes sport the red dragon, right, but the earliest cask labels, left, carry the three feathers.

It's Brains You Want

Brains did not have to rack their brains hard to come up with a striking slogan. Nor did the brewery need to employ specialist marketing consultants. They just let the staff provide the inspiration.

Mrs E. George claimed in 1981 that she had coined the familiar words 'It's Brains You Want', while working as a young barmaid at the Canton Hotel just after World War One. And a painter and signwriter at the brewery in around 1900, Albert Jones, is said to have devised the enlarged 'AI' in Brains, which came to adorn many of their pub walls and windows.

But the most striking image was a howling dog. In the 1920s local rivals Hancock's commissioned a series of posters. Instead of the usual plea to 'Drink XYZ Ale', these used humour to sell with a smile. One popular poster by artist Lawson Wood in 1924 featured a sailor on the beach knocking back a bottle of beer, with a little bucket-and-spade girl asking, 'Please may I have a look through your telescope?'.

Brains bit back with the telling tale of an unfortunate mongrel. The mutt was shown howling in pain after a full crate of Brains

bottled beer had fallen off a brewery dray on to its tail, beneath the punning slogan 'Brain's Honest Ale' (say it quickly). The moving mural appeared on walls and pubs across town. You couldn't fail to see the joke. The one on The Halfway in Cathedral Road was almost half the height of the hotel, right.

The last one was still yelping on the bricks in Bute Street in the 1970s. The city council even considered saving the fading landmark and moving it to a new location as part of Cardiff's contribution to European Heritage Year in 1974.

The mangy mongrel was finally put down in 1981 when the wall near the Salvation Army hostel was demolished. But then the persistent little terrier barked back from the dead in Womanby Street on the side of Dempseys for a while, after the Four Bars Inn was turned into an Irish-themed pub in 1995.

Despite his long-suffering tail, the dog was not Brains official trade mark, but it took a long while for the distinctive Red Dragon to scorch his fiery features across the Brains brand. The 'AI' symbol was initially preferred, with

the Red Dragon name instead adopted for Brains' best-selling beer, Dark. A 19th Century cask label flaunted the Prince of Wales' feathers rather than a dragon, while some early bottle labels featured a jovial landlord pouring glasses of beer.

But gradually the Red Dragon began to stamp itself across all of Brains beers. A crude sketch was used on early promotional items like two different coloured snuff boxes. The mythical beast was sharpened up for the bottle labels and then slowly evolved over the years, developing a more

50

The most striking image was a howling dog

upright stance from the late 1950s. The most revolutionary change came in 2003, when a more dynamic dragon was turned round to face right instead of left.

But the Red Dragon largely missed out on two of the brewery's other main ways of spreading the Brains name across the streets of Cardiff.

OFF COLOUR

A poster was produced for Brains Red Dragon early in the 20th century. But it was clearly the work of an artist who had never seen the beer, for he envisaged gleaming glasses of a golden pale ale instead of the Dark known and loved in Cardiff.

Selling on the Streets

Brains did not go in for large-scale newspaper advertising. Apart from the top corner of the front page of the *Western Mail*, the brewery kept a low profile in the press for many years, while occasionally splashing out in local sports and other programmes.

But besides decorating its own pubs, it kept the brewery firmly in the public eye by stretching its name across Cardiff's main roads. Many of the approaches to the city centre ducked under railway bridges, and you could not pass through without coming under the influence of Brains, whose beers were prominently displayed on almost every span.

The Bute Street bridge, right, advertising Brains Strong Ale in the 1960s, was so heavily powerful, weighing down on the road below, it almost seemed about to crush anyone from the docks trying to squeeze underneath to reach The Glastonbury, The Golden Cross or The Salutation on the other side.

Besides these solid-steel displays, Brains also helped to keep its reputation rolling along the streets by advertising on

buses and trams, with its beers plastered across the sides of many double-deckers – which led to a long-running dispute.

Dry campaigners on Cardiff Council managed to ban all drinks advertising on trams and buses in 1923. The issue came to a head nine years later, when the council's tramways committee also tried to stop pub advertising on the back of tickets.

'We're rather tired of the continued attempts to use the council chamber as the medium for furthering teetotal propaganda, much of which in the past has made Cardiff the laughing stock of the country,' complained The Cardiff Licensed Victuallers' Association.

South Wales Echo cartoonist, J.C. Walker, produced a sketch of one of the leading dry campaigners, Rev Penry Thomas, looking distinctly uncomfortable, above, sitting in an empty tram surrounded by beer posters, including the half-hidden slogan 'It's Brains You Want' behind his head.

The full council then overruled the committee's decision. Alderman Sir Illtyd Thomas said the 'Drys' were inconsistent in their arguments. In London beers and stouts

were advertised on public transport, but he had never heard of the teetotal members walking when they were in the city. The drinks advertising ban on the buses was heading for the terminus of no return and was repealed in June 1932.

But the authorities did restrict all prominent promotions on the sides of buildings and bridges after World War Two, resulting in the disappearance of many well-known Brains landmarks, although some later reappeared as the rules were relaxed.

BRAINS

STRONG ALE

Brains kept in the public eye by stretching its name across Cardiff's main roads

S.A. BRAIN & Co LTD
TRADE MARK
OLD BREWERY
CARDIFF
STRONG ALE

BITTER EXPERIENCE

A haulage driver from Leeds had a bitter experience in Cardiff in 1996 when transporting a huge tank from Yorkshire to Barry. His load became jammed under the railway bridge on Cowbridge Road. And directly above the stuck vehicle, Brains had painted the weighty word 'Bitter'. His company certainly was, as it blamed Cardiff Council for recommending the wrong route. The council said the driver had become lost.

Red Dragon was the toast and taste of the capital

IT'S A
BRAINS BREW

RED DRAGON
the draught beer of quality

Drinking in the Dark

Songs in honour of Cardiff always seem to rhyme Cardiff Arms Park with Brains Dark. It was the first and second pints after work, the first and seventh pints after the rugby match and the prime lubrication for male voice choirs. It flowed over the bars in the capital and was soaked into the streets. It was the beer on which Brains was built.

Dark left all the other draught beers in the shade. It dominated production at The Old Brewery, even in the country's darkest hour. An old stock ledger shows that on 30 September 1940 out of 1,579 barrels at the brewery, RD (Red Dragon) accounted for 1,155 barrels. The next most popular beer was IPA with 213 barrels, followed by LB (Light Bitter) on just 138.

Though the beer's official title was Red Dragon, it was always known in Cardiff as 'Dark'. Eventually the brewery also adopted this name. Brains Bitter was often called 'Light'. The tasty ale so symbolised the business, that the Red Dragon became the company's trademark.

S.A. Brain, whose initials were later linked to the brewery's premium beer, had not intended to rely on this mighty mild trade. Alfred Barnard, on a visit in the late 1880s, commented, 'Messrs Brain & Co have now become so proficient in the art of brewing pale ales that the Cardiff publicans are not obliged to go to the "beer city" for their Burton ales, since that commodity is now being brewed on the very same principle in their own town'.

S.A. Brain was hoping to capture the invading English brewers' more profitable business in premium beers. Barnard approved: 'We sampled two or three sorts – pale ale, mild beer and stout.

A *capital* drink

I·P·A
IT'S A
BRAINS BREW

RARE MIXTURE

One Brains pub, the Crown at Skewen, near Neath, offered Brains MA, a brewery mixture of Dark and Bitter, as the locals preferred a darker bitter.

After the GAME Say SA BRAIN'S BEST BITTER

S.W. Echo 13/9/58

The first we found to be a delicious, full-flavoured tonic beverage; the latter a nutritious well-bodied drink.' The mild passed his lips without comment. But it was the beer Cardiff's workers demanded.

It was drunk by young and old, men and women, and not just cold. David Jones of Splott recalled that he had his first taste of Dark in 1927 at the age of seven. 'My grandmother used to send me out when I was young to get a jug filled up with ale. She would then mull it with a hot poker and give me a sip. But the sips just got bigger and bigger.'

Until the early 1980s, Dark was Brains' best-selling ale by far. It sold much more than all the brewery's other beers combined. Some Cardiff pubs, like the Railway Inn in Fairwater, sold only Dark on draught until as late as 1980.

Though its strength was sapped by two world wars, the pump clip declares it is still 'brewed to the original recipe'. 'It's a fine blend of pale ale and roasted chocolate malts, Goldings and Fuggles hops from Worcestershire – and Welsh water,' enthused Head Brewer John Glazzard in 1991. 'There should be rings of lacing down the glass, showing how many gulps the drinker has taken.'

Unlike most other dark milds, which are usually sweet, Brains Dark is distinctively dry, having the same units of bitterness as the brewery's bitter. It has a refreshing, roasted aroma and spicy flavour, with hints of coffee. 'I can say quite objectively that Dark is on its own,' added John Glazzard. 'It is unique.'

Cardiff drinkers certainly agreed. It was the toast and taste of the capital. Even when they chose another brew, it was often as a mix with Dark. A price list from the brewery in April 1959 listed Red Dragon, Bitter and "Half Red Dragon and Half Bitter" all at 1s 1d a pint. Only SA at 1s 3d was more expensive.

The beer was the Dark heart of Brains for most of its history.

The brewery bottled its own brands such as Mount Stuart and Glendu Scotch, Barock Irish Whiskey and Sherdale British Sherry

Spirits in the Brewery

Besides beer, most pubs also came to sell the pint's natural chaser – spirits. And as sales grew, so breweries became increasingly interested in a drop of gin, rum or whisky.

S.A. Brain tried to ensure he had his fingers round every glass by becoming chairman of Cardiff wine and spirits merchants Stevens and Sons, founded around 1850, which was converted into a limited company in 1889. Its business rivalled the brewery's in size.

The firm had substantial premises in St Mary Street, reaching back to Westgate Street, as well as additional bonded stores at Canal Side in Bute Dock and in the Rotunda Buildings in Penarth Road. In the 1890s the Rotunda was said to contain 'the largest single bonded cellar' outside London, 150 feet long by 66 feet wide, while the three-storey Canal Side premises, which were devoted solely to whisky, contained a hydraulic lift 'capable of raising one ton'. Leading brands included Edinbro' Cream and Duchess Scotch.

However, this close connection in St Mary Street was not to last. In 1896 Stevens and Sons was taken over by Brains' main brewing rivals in Cardiff, Hancock's, who were on a spending spree funded by repeated issues of shares. Brains could not compete; it did not become a limited company until the following year. Edinbro' Cream and Duchess became Hancock's brands.

At this time, extremely strong 'over-proofed' spirits were often provided to pubs in small casks, the licensee then needing to 'reduce' the liquor to the correct alcoholic level. Since this was a skilled task, requiring careful calculations and the use of a hydrometer, variations in strength often occurred. As legislation was tightened up in World War One and duty sharply increased, it became essential to ensure the calculations were correct. Too potent spirits could easily have everyone staggering into trouble.

After the war, Brains decided to bring its wine and spirits trade in-house to carry out this work in controlled conditions. With the demolition of the original brewery buildings in 1919, this created space at The Old Brewery for the new Wines and Spirits Department.

Tom Black, who became head of the department in 1921, initiated a new policy where the department bought all the wines and spirits centrally and distributed them to Brains pubs. Previously, landlords had bought their own supplies independently from various sources.

SPIRITS REVIVED

The 21st century has seen a bold revival of Brains' links with spirits in Wales, for the brewery provides the malted barley wash for The Welsh Whisky Company, near Hirwaun, which launched Penderyn single malt in 2004. The 8 per cent all-malt brew is the basis for the first whisky to be produced in Wales since 1894.

In addition to well-known brands such as Johnnie Walker and Teachers, the brewery also bottled its own brands, such as Mount Stuart and Glendu Scotch, Barock Irish Whiskey and Sherdale British Sherry. These were bought in bulk by Brains and then filtered, diluted to the appropriate strength and blended and coloured where necessary at the brewery, before being bottled.

After World War Two, however, the public began increasingly to call for the heavily-advertised national brands, despite the brewery instructing its landlords that 'The sales of our own proprietary brands must be encouraged'.

'As this trend continued it became progressively less worthwhile to supply the brewery's own brands, and harder to bottle economically on such a small scale,' the company later admitted.

In 1973 the bottling plant was removed and three years later Brains joined a consortium of 26 other independent breweries, called Clansouth, which could negotiate better discounts from major suppliers of wines and spirits.

Only the lingering aroma of Mount Stuart and the other Brains spirits was left to haunt The Old Brewery's twisting corridors.

Brains' wines and spirits price list, left, from 1926.

57

Brains, with shares closely controlled by the family, was determined to remain independent

Land of the Giants

On a freezing cold day in February 1961, three car loads of passengers risked the danger of heavy snowfalls to meet not far from the Grouse Inn at Hayfield, near Kinder Scout, high up in the Peak District of Derbyshire. Hidden behind a stone wall, they ate a cold lunch.

But this was no winter picnic. Inside the cars were representatives from three major breweries: Brigadier Noel Tetley and Thomas Walker of the newly-formed Tetley-Walker of Leeds and Liverpool, Edward Thompson and Gerald Thorley of Ind Coope of Burton and Romford and Archibald Wiley and Garnet Cornwell from Ansells of Birmingham.

Meeting on the moors in secret to discuss a massive merger, they were planning to combine their individual strengths in the North, Midlands and South of England into one national brewing group. They soon warmed to their task and an agreement was hammered out. Ind Coope Tetley Ansell Ltd was formed in May 1961, changing its name to Allied Breweries two years later. The new land of the giants was born.

The swinging 60s was to see a large scythe sweep through the brewing industry, as the new 'Big Six' of Allied Breweries, Bass Charrington, Courage, Scottish & Newcastle, Watney and Whitbread took over and cut down independent local breweries across the UK. The decade was also to shake up the beer trade in South Wales, until the froth flew.

In a rush to fund expansion in the past, many local companies had sold shares widely. Now they were vulnerable to takeover. They had lost control and often could only decide into whose arms to jump.

The king of the coalfields, Rhymney Breweries, which had itself taken over Crosswells of Cardiff in 1936 and then Ely Brewery in 1959, had enjoyed close connections with Whitbread since 1951. The London brewer had directors on the Rhymney board and a share stake. Rhymney was the first to shelter under what became known as 'the Whitbread umbrella'. It offered protection against outside predators – except, of course, Whitbread. The hind's head galloped away with the hobby horse brewers in 1966, also swallowing another mining brewer, Evan Evans Bevan of Neath, the following year, to form Whitbread Wales.

Brains' close rival Hancock's could not escape the grasp of the giants either. Like Rhymney, it had close connections that proved costly in the end. Hancock's had strode across South Wales by taking over a grand total of 17 breweries. The last, David Roberts and Sons in 1960, expanded its Welsh empire as far as Aberystwyth.

Hancock's was the Welsh giant, with 500 pubs, but compared to the new combines it was small beer. Bass Charrington boasted 11,000 pubs. Hancock's had long trading links with Bass, and in 1968 the Burton brewers took over, creating a new company, Welsh Brewers, in Cardiff, which combined

Hancock's former brewery now became the heart of Bass' operations in Wales, trading as Welsh Brewers.

Hancock's with the Fernvale Brewery and Webbs of Aberbeeg.

Hancock's chairman Joseph Gaskell, who became chairman of Welsh Brewers, had two years earlier hinted at the thinking behind the merger when he said that the future would be difficult, 'especially for smaller companies which going it alone cannot achieve great economies of scale'.

But Brains, under the Chairmanship of Michael Brain, continued to ensure that shares were closely controlled by the family, which was determined to remain fully independent. However, it was now left isolated in Cardiff in a much more hostile environment. Instead of competing against slightly larger local rivals like Rhymney and Hancock's, it now faced the might of British giants like Whitbread and Bass head on.

There were challenging times ahead.

FIGHTING GOLIATH

A *Financial Times* survey in the late 1980s indicated the scale of the challenge facing Brains after the 1960s. It found Brains had 7 per cent of the South Wales beer market compared to Bass' massive 40 per cent through Welsh Brewers. Whitbread Wales, with 15 per cent, had more than double Brains' trade.

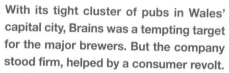

Heart of the Capital

With its tight cluster of pubs in Wales' capital city, Brains was a tempting target for the major brewers. But the company stood firm, helped by a consumer revolt.

The arrival of the new national combines was inevitably followed by the introduction of national brands. Each one of the Big Six rolled out heavily-promoted brews, like Allied's Double Diamond, Courage Tavern, Worthington E from Bass, Younger's Tartan, Watney's Red and Whitbread Tankard. Brains could not compete in this multi-million pound marketing world. Its own keg beers, Gold Dragon and Tudor Light, failed to fizz.

These processed 'keg' beers often replaced local, naturally-conditioned cask beers, much to the disgust of many local drinkers. A consumer movement, CAMRA, the Campaign for Real Ale, sprang up in response in the early 1970s and it generated demand for local real ales. Under Bill Rhys, appointed Chairman in 1971 to succeed the late Michael Brain, The Old Brewery faced a new problem.

Instead of being under threat, the company was struggling to keep up with demand. The brewers were even ejected from their office to make way for an extra fermenting vessel. But emergency measures like this were only a short-term answer. Even the transfer of some draught beer production to The New Brewery in Roath, after a decline in the bottled beer trade, could only absorb part of the surge in demand.

In 1975 Brains decided to cement its place in the heart and hearts of the capital through a major £2.8 million expansion of The Old Brewery. It was a huge expression of faith in the future. It was also to prove a long and painful operation lasting seven years, since brewing and deliveries had to continue throughout the redevelopment.

One sign of the changing times was that the neighbouring Tabernacl Welsh Baptist church allowed access through its yard for part of the work to be carried out. The old teetotal preachers must have spun in their graves.

Two new stainless steel mash tuns and two coppers were among the vessels installed, while a new fermentation tower had to be given a quality, glazed finish so that it fitted in with the smart city centre skyline, looking like a small office building. The old brick chimney, built in 1934, was replaced by a thin, silver stack.

By late 1979 the essential work was complete, increasing capacity by 50 per cent or an extra 18 million pints a year. But work then began on upgrading the cellars beneath the yard. The relief of the staff when this was finally completed can be gauged by a report in *The Brewer* magazine. 'Eventually, by early 1982, the redevelopment was more or less complete, and a vigorous campaign to evict the contractors – who had taken root – was undertaken.'

Every inch of the cramped site had been used. Even the flat roof of the fermentation block had been designed with a surrounding rail so it could be used to store casks. And now this exercise in claustrophobic engineering was over, just in time to celebrate the centenary of S.A. Brain's takeover of The Old Brewery in 1882.

But it was a time to look forward rather than back. It was time for Brains to make the most of its increased brewing capacity by selling more barrels. And for that the company needed to look beyond Cardiff.

Brains decided to cement its place in the heart and hearts of the capital through a £2.8 million expansion of The Old Brewery

TIME CHECK

The redevelopment of the brewery had given curious Cardiff a glimpse inside Brains. As buildings were demolished in Caroline Street at the side, passers-by could clearly see the brewery clock, which had been peering down from the top of the 1887 brewhouse since 1926. When the work was completed, this welcome time check disappeared again.

Peter Lewis checks the time on the brewery clock.

Lost and Saved

Pubs that had survived the war were now being demolished across Cardiff – with one shining exception

If there was substantial change at the brewery, a violent revolution had been sweeping the streets outside. Many pubs that had survived the war and then welcomed the return of Sunday trading with open doors in 1961 were now being demolished across Cardiff.

Many areas of the city were being redeveloped, and as the back-to-back houses were cleared the small community pubs they contained were also reduced to rubble. The Little Ireland of Newtown was completely flattened in 1967, along with locals like The Crichton Arms, The Cambridge and The Duke of Edinburgh. In Canton a whole host of community pubs were lost when the Wellington Street area was redeveloped in 1975, including Brains' Red Cow and the Duke of York.

Others were steam-rollered by the big stores as they surged across the city centre. Queen Street became a dry desert. Well-known pubs like The Tivoli in 1960 and The Taff Vale in 1977 were closed to make way for shopping developments, as was the Marchioness of Bute. Yet more familiar landmarks, like The Rose and Crown on

Kingsway, were driven underground as roads were widened.

The pub seemed to be under threat from all sides, but occasionally a successful stand was made against the destructive drive of the bulldozer.

The Golden Cross is one of the iconic pubs of Cardiff. Standing at the top of Bute Street, gazing down into the docks from the edge of the city centre, it occupies a strategic site. Its walls have also embraced much of the capital's colourful history, including magnificent tiled murals of Cardiff Castle and the old Town Hall, besides a glorious green and gold glazed bar.

The present Golden Cross was built in 1904 and offered a lively night on the tiles for sailors off the ships. During the war American servicemen enjoyed the pub's delights. One young GI is alleged to have swung his first fist in anger during a fight in the bar. His name was Rocky Marciano.

In 1978 it seemed this flawed gem was about to disappear when South Glamorgan County Council proposed to drive a road through the site. But a vigorous campaign by Brains, the *South Wales Echo* and the

All gone - The Duke of York, left, and The Marchioness of Bute, below, were both demolished, while The Wyndham, above, was turned into offices.

Cardiff branch of CAMRA stopped the plan in its tracks.

Brains said it would spend £100,000 restoring the pub to its former glory. The final cost was four times that amount. When work began, it was discovered that the famous boozer was unsteady on its feet. It had been built without proper foundations, so the whole building had to be underpinned and the back walls rebuilt. A heavy cast-iron bay window on the first floor also had to be removed. Only then could

VOCAL SUPPORT

After The Golden Cross reopened, left and below, Tom Jones added his voice of approval by singing in the bar in 1987, along with the Treorchy Male Voice Choir, for an HTV Christmas special. Between songs, Brains beer kept his vocal chords well lubricated, and afterwards he signed many autographs in the heaving pub. Landlord Adrian Price said it had been 'absolute murder' keeping the surprise appearance secret.

specialist companies be brought in to restore damaged tiles, while a new bar that had once been a counter at Cardiff's old central post office in Westgate Street was added at one end.

'The refurbishment of the Golden Cross is the most complicated operation of its kind that the company has ever undertaken,' said Brains' Estates Manager Ian Richards when the pub finally reopened in 1986. The restoration won the Prince of Wales Award for service to the community, the first time a pub had received this honour.

But The Golden Cross was a shining exception in a bleak sea of rubble. Many of Brains' surrounding pubs, like The Salutation, The Custom House and The Glendower, were lost. Even the famous Glastonbury was bulldozed in the early 1990s, despite its distinctive 1920s façade by architect Sir Percy Thomas, which had earned it the title of 'The White House' among seamen around the world.

'TWO LLAGERS PLEASE, TAFFY'

Barrels of Laughs!

Cartoonists have often found themselves strangely drawn towards Brains, particularly local legend Gren (Grenville Jones), who regularly featured the brewery and its pubs in his cartoons in the *South Wales Echo*.

"DON'T PANIC, MR BRAIN'S NOT GOING TO SELL THEM THE BLOODY LOT!"

A Bear of Very Little Brains....

'I'm all for Lord Neil reffin' the game, it's Rhodri an' Nick Bourne runnin' the lines worries me.'

"Ah, Mr Brain, come in, great! Me an' the team have come up with a few more posters to upset your English customers."

IN WALES. ITS BEEN REFRESHING THE PARTS THAT HEINEKEN CANT EVEN SPELL, LOK YEARS.

Brains Bitter now ruled the handpumps, selling nearly three times as much as Dark

Brewing Change

The major upheavals in the brewhouse and the pub estate were reflected in the mix of beers on sale at the bar. The once dominant beer, Dark, was becoming a shadow of its former self. During the 1980s, it was eclipsed by the Light.

Brains Bitter now ruled the handpumps, selling nearly three times as much as Dark. By 1991 it accounted for 57 per cent of production, compared to 20 per cent for Dark. It was the prime 'session' beer – the one that kept Cardiff drinkers going back to the bar for another pint.

But the new flagship beer was SA. Brains had always produced a best bitter, under the name IPA, to compete with Burton pale ales like Bass, but sales had not taken off. After World War Two, the brewery in 1949 launched a new brew called Extra as 'the better bitter on draught', but it failed to fly.

In the mid-1950s Brains tried again with SA Best Bitter. Drinkers abbreviated the bar call to SA and the beer was soon linked to Samuel Arthur Brain's initials – and struck a chord at the counter. In 1991, whilst the barrelage was still below Dark, accounting for 17 per cent of total production, its reputation was much, much bigger. It became popularly known as 'Skull Attack', though its alcoholic strength of 4.2 per cent was not staggering. It became the most famous Brains beer, the one that drinkers far from Cardiff could instantly recall.

But while traditional cask ales dominated production at The Old Brewery, the national combines were promoting a very different type of beer. After marketing keg ales at first, they had turned their attention to lager. Brews like Harp from Guinness, Skol from Allied Breweries, Carling Black Label from Bass and Heineken from Whitbread now mopped up the lion's share of their advertising budgets. By 1985 lager sales had frothed up to 40 per cent of the British beer trade.

Brains decided it was a market it could not ignore. Its keg ales under its own name, Gold Dragon and Tudor Light, promoted by a cartoon dragon, had failed to roar, being replaced by Capital Keg in 1981. Lager drinkers expected something more exotic. They were getting used to 'continental' brands like Carlsberg, so Brains scoured Europe for a suitable brew.

Eventually, in conjunction with the Eldridge Pope brewery in Dorset, it settled on another family brewery, Faust of Miltenberg in Bavaria. It was a costly adventure. More than £1.5 million was spent on converting The New Brewery in Roath for lager production, including installing eight conical fermenting vessels. The yeast was flown in from southern Germany every month.

Faust was launched at the height of summer in 1985. On 29 July more than 200 pubs and clubs around Cardiff turned on the taps to serve the Teutonic tipple. Within a year, Brains was celebrating the 100th brew. 'Sales have exceeded all our expectations,' said joint managing director Christopher Brain.

But after the initial froth of excitement, Faust (meaning fist in German) could not match the punching power of the major lager brands, with their million-pound marketing budgets. Faust was withdrawn in 1991, but Brains continued to brew lager.

END OF THE LINE

Once lager went flat, Brains' New Brewery was closed in 1993, along with its bottling and canning lines. This brought to an end the brewery's brief attempt to sell its ales to supermarkets in large, plastic bottles for the take-home trade, alongside cans of Brains 'Bavarian Lager'. The New Brewery was demolished in 1995. It had failed to outlast The Old.

Since 1986 it had also brewed the premium Swiss lager Hurlimann under licence, again in conjunction with another English family brewery – Shepherd Neame of Kent. But the Zurich brew had to compete with another 'star' brand at the bar – Stella Artois – after a trading agreement with Whitbread in 1990. Hurlimann was outgunned and by 1993 Brains' foray into lager brewing was over.

BRAINS TAKE-HO[ME] RANGE OF BEERS AND LAGER.

Brains made a substantial bricks and mortar commitment to business across the border

Invading England

One of the elusive Holy Grails of the brewing industry in Wales had been to establish a market across the border. Scottish brewers had succeeded in invading England; brands like McEwan's Export and Younger's Tartan were as well known in London as Edinburgh. Ireland was blessed with the king of stout Guinness. But Welsh ales rarely crossed English lips, except when they were visiting The Principality.

A few brewers had tried – and failed. Hancock's in 1946 had opened a depot in Dudley in the West Midlands, but the Cardiff ales never captivated Black Country tastes and within five years the venture was abandoned. Only Felinfoel near Llanelli had a brand that breathed fire across the border, after Double Dragon won the Challenge Cup for the best cask beer at the Brewers Exhibition in London in 1976.

Brains' business was so concentrated in Cardiff that it barely extended far beyond the capital, never mind across the border. There was also little scope for expansion, as the brewery could sell locally almost every pint it could squeeze

out of its compact city centre site. There was even rationing at Christmas.

But with the new brewhouse completed in 1982, there was extra capacity to fill. Now Brains had to focus on selling beer outside its traditional markets. For the first time a marketing department was set up in 1984 under Tony Smith, who had recently been employed at Express Dairies. Advertising and sponsorship were increased, including the Mallett Cup in rugby, the Welsh Football League Challenge Cup in football and Brains International Matchplay in darts.

A guide to Brains' 125 houses was introduced, along with a passport scheme, where drinkers completing a circuit of pubs would receive a pewter tankard. 'I budgeted for 20, but in the end had to send out 650,' admitted Tony Smith. 'The response was amazing. We got the first complete passport back in two weeks.'

A shop was opened at the front of The Old Brewery in St Mary Street in 1984, selling a variety of products from T-shirts to tankards. Demand for goods carrying the famous slogan 'It's Brains You Want' flooded in from around the world.

SA was launched in cans in 1989 and soon accounted for almost half of all Brains' take-home sales. The packaged brew won a silver medal at the Brewing Industry International Awards the following year. In 1990, Brains struck a trading agreement with Whitbread, allowing the national brewer's tenants to stock Brains Dark and Bitter. The profile of the brewery was further lifted in 1991, when Brains Dark was named Champion Mild Ale at the Great British Beer Festival in London. Brains beers were beginning to travel much more widely.

The same year the company made a substantial bricks and mortar commitment to business across the border. Brains launched a marina development just outside Bath which included a new pub, The Boathouse,

above and left. It had already developed a reputation for its beers in the West Country spa thanks to a long-standing link with the Royal Oak at Larkhall, which became known as The Brains Surgery. The opening of The Boathouse was packed with celebrities. Tory party chairman and local MP Chris Patten planted a tree, while actors Timothy West and his wife Prunella Scales, right, toasted the venture with Christopher Brain as they moored their narrowboat in one of the 60 berths.

Building on this move, Brains now has around 10 per cent of its tied estate in England. But the brewery was not neglecting its backyard. Major projects were also planned for Cardiff.

EUROPEAN ADVENTURES

Drinkers abroad could even occasionally pick up a Brains beer. In 1988 the brewery exported its IPA as Old Brewery Special Bitter 'bier de luxe' to France. The first 1,296 dozen bottles were targeted at Brittany as the region shared a common Celtic culture.

HET BIER VAN WALES

BRAINS

BRAINS OLD BREWERY SPECIAL BITTER

Bier
DE LUXE

BREWED IN THE U.K. BY S.A. BRAIN & CO. LTD. CARDIFF

The colourful bricks were specially made from an imperial Victorian mould. The floors were even built to creak

Capital Projects

The transformation of the city's run-down docks into Cardiff Bay was one of the largest urban development projects in Europe, and Brains was determined to play its part with an equally grand scheme – The Wharf.

Set alongside Bute East Dock, close to the new County Hall, the impressive development was one of the most ambitious projects ever undertaken by an independent brewer when it opened in 1991.

It was designed in two parts. Looking out across the new urban lake were two waterside bars and a restaurant, while a second three-storey building contained studio offices and shops. Linking the two was a glass atrium covering a reconstructed railway station to provide a platform of fun for children using the adjoining family room.

The impressive newly-built structure was in the style of a bonded warehouse and looked as if it had been standing for at least a century. The building was on a grand scale, with metal columns and wrought-iron balconies. The timber used was reclaimed from old buildings, while the colourful bricks were specially made from an imperial

Victorian mould. The floors were even built to creak.

The scent of the sea was carried inside by portraits of famous Cardiff shipping magnates, freshly painted by artist Andrew Taylor, but looking like Victorian oil paintings. An imposing statue of a docker by sculptor Chris Kelly dominated the entrance, while a huge ship owners' banner by Frankie Lane of Barry, featuring sailing ships, the Pierhead building and Brains' Old Brewery, took pride of place in the restaurant. A boathouse was also built nearby for Cardiff Boat Club.

With the marina development in Bath the same year, The Wharf, opened by Welsh Office minister David Hunt, symbolised Brains' ambition to develop its business.

Another significant investment in 1991 saw the company open its first major hotel, Churchills in Llandaff. The renovation of the former 33-bedroom Victorian hotel included a new function suite and nine mews cottages. And Brains followed up this move by buying a second hotel, The Lamb & Flag in Abergavenny.

These were all huge projects, but a much bigger development was on its way.

TROUBLED WATERS

Brains' launch of The Wharf was not all plain sailing. The brewery originally bought an old Bristol Channel pilot cutter, *The Mascotte*, to moor alongside the bars – only to discover the plan had been left high and dry. The water was too shallow to take the boat after developers dumped masses of rubble into the docks unannounced, sharply reducing the depth. So Brains instead had to settle for a flat-bottomed 75-foot Dutch barge, the *Ebenhaezer*.

Crown Buckley
provided a perfect fit

Some Momentous Night

'I was driving home at four o'clock in the morning by myself and the blackbirds had just started to sing and I thought, crikey, we've just acquired Crown Buckley,' recalled Chairman Christopher Brain. 'That was some momentous night. That day at 11 o'clock we had our AGM, so it was all fairly tight scheduled stuff.'

The deal, which surprised the industry early in March 1997, was the result of secret nocturnal meetings. 'You wouldn't wish it to leak out because it would have unsettled the customers, the managers, the tenants and the free trade as to who was going to provide their beer.

'I think that is fairly common practice on acquisitions. It's the lawyers who seem to like working into the early hours of the morning. You'd be surprised at how the adrenalin keeps you going.'

The takeover was fresh territory for Brains. Unlike its Cardiff neighbours Hancock's, which had swallowed 18 breweries in less than 80 years, Brains ploughed its own furrow and the only brewery it had ever bought was Watson's

Cambrian Brewery in Womanby Street more than a century before in 1885.

'Acquiring other companies was not something that was considered. If anything, we were fending off predators coming in making enquiries as to whether we wished to sell out,' said Christopher Brain.

But Brains was seeking to build up its trade and pub estate and Crown Buckley provided a perfect fit, since Brains was dominant in Cardiff while Crown Buckley's core market was in the mining valleys and West Wales. Brains was strong in tied pubs, while Crown Buckley had a greater presence in the free trade, particularly clubs.

Crown Buckley had been created in 1988 through the merger of the United Clubs Brewery of Pontyclun and Buckley's Brewery of Llanelli. The acquisition included 28 pubs, taking Brains estate up to 165, as well as an historic brewery at Llanelli and a packaging plant at Pontyclun. And there was an option to buy more pubs. Crown Buckley became a

subsidiary within Brains, called Brain Crown Buckley Ltd.

The takeover created a Welsh brewing giant, with an annual turnover of £60 million. Brains was now in a stronger position to compete with the major British breweries. 'The UK brewing industry has become a very competitive market place, particularly for independent brewers. In order to compete with the majors a regional brewer needs to be of a certain critical size,' added Christopher Brain.

But Brains had not only swelled in size, it had also swallowed a company with a long and colourful history.

Chairman Christopher Brain celebrates the merger with Mike Salter, right, of Crown Buckley.

S·A·BRAIN & Co. LTD.

. BRAIN & Co LTD
HE OLD BREWERY
T MARY STREET
CARDIFF
TEL:01222 399022,
TARY R.C. MAY-HILL, F.C.A.

CROWN BUCKLEY

FL6 18

HUGE POTENTIAL

Brains' Group Chief Executive, Richard May-Hill, said 'Concluding an agreement of this sort demands a huge effort from the respective parties. However, although we regard this as an historic moment, it is importantly the starting point for future development. We will now be devoting all our energies to making sure that we fulfil the potential which these new arrangements promise.'

The Gospel and The Glass

Part of Brains' range of beers today, The Rev. James, illustrates just how closely the gospel and the glass were once connected in Wales. And the liquid links flow far beyond Reverend James Buckley to the man who originally founded Buckley's Brewery in Llanelli.

Henry Child was not only a remarkable entrepreneur, but also a leading Methodist. He came to Llanelli in 1760 as an estate agent, and within nine years had leased The Talbot's Head Inn and then The Falcon, as well as running an old malt house. He was also involved in farming and flour mills. After obtaining another two pubs, in 1799 he leased a central site to erect a brewery. Yet at the same time he built the town's first Methodist chapel, Wind Street Chapel, in his own garden in 1792.

Methodist leader John Wesley often stayed in his home, as did other itinerant preachers including the Rev. James Buckley from Lancashire, who married Henry Child's daughter, Maria, in 1798. When Henry Child died in 1824, James Buckley found himself with two concerns to run – saving souls and satisfying thirsts.

The pint and the pulpit had never been so close.

When he died in 1839, while attending the Methodist Centenary Conference in Liverpool, his body was brought back to Llanelli and buried in the parish church – just across the road from the expanding brewery.

His son, also called James Buckley, took over the business. He was a single-

DANGEROUS CROSSING

The Rev. James Buckley almost never stamped his family name on the Llanelli brewery. In 1794, while attempting to reach the town, he tried to wade across a small arm of the sea. But the water was too deep and the current far too strong, and he was swept away for a quarter-of-mile before reaching the other shore. Even then he was stuck in soft mud, until an onlooker guided and pulled him to safety. Later a Buckley's pub, The Reverend James, was built in Loughor, to mark the escape.

minded, stern Victorian businessman, who built up the company. He commanded respect, even fear. When his son-in-law, who managed a local bank, suffered a run on the bank, James Buckley called out one of the brewery drays. Then he marched in procession with his staff to the besieged building, where gold bars were unloaded and carried into the vaults. The crisis was ended.

His unyielding character, however, could create enemies. The manager of the brewery, William Bythway, long complained about his pay and conditions. Making no headway, he switched tactics and then proposed to James Buckley's daughter, but was bluntly rejected. So in 1875, he left and set up his own brewery.

The move was later to come back to haunt his two sons, James and William Joseph Buckley, who took over from their father in 1883, trading as Buckley Brothers.

THE REV. JAMES

A TASTE OF THE GOOD LIFE

The Rev. James

ABV 4.5%

S.A. BRAIN & Cº LIMITED CARDIFF WALES

Traditional Beer from Wales

CWRW TRADDODIADOL O GYMRU

IT'S BRAINS YOU WANT

Buckley's was firmly established as the brewing giant of South-West Wales with 250 pubs

Rulers of the West

Immediately after leaving Brains in Cardiff in 1890, brewery chronicler Alfred Barnard headed straight for Llanelli by train. 'Our only reason for staying a couple of days in the town was to inspect Messrs Buckley's great brewery, which we found full of animation and business.'

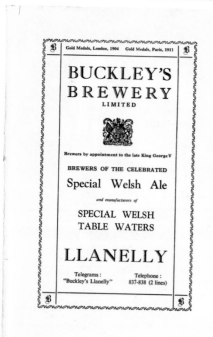

Gold Medals, London, 1904   Gold Medals, Paris, 1911

BUCKLEY'S BREWERY
LIMITED

Brewers by appointment to the late King George V

BREWERS OF THE CELEBRATED
Special Welsh Ale
and manufacturers of
SPECIAL WELSH TABLE WATERS

LLANELLY

Telegrams :   Telephone :
"Buckley's Llanelly"   837-838 (2 lines)

It dominated the town, with extensive maltings as well as a brewhouse. 'All the buildings are lofty and most substantially constructed.'

The extent of the trade can be seen from the fact that the cellars contained 'nearly 7,000 barrels of ale'. But the gospel and the glass were no longer comfortable partners. Buckley's had been under increasing pressure from the chapel-led temperance movement. A trip to the sample cellar quickly loosened Barnard's tongue in defence of beer.

'Ale is certainly the best and cheapest drink that a working man can take. Tea, coffee and new milk are all higher priced than beer. Excellent beer, like that we tasted, is especially suited for those hard workers, foundry men, miners and engineers who abound in this populous district. It can be obtained at threepence the quart, and forms a better article of drink with their solid food than tea.'

When the brewery was launched as a limited company in 1894, the business was valued at £162,350 with 120 pubs, with trade stretching from Tenby and Newcastle Emlyn to Maesteg. And it was soon to expand further through two major takeovers, though Buckley's was stung by its first purchase.

After manager William Bythway had left Buckley's under a cloud in 1875, he had set up The New Brewery in Llanelli. Now he was looking to sell up, but refusing to supply firm figures. Buckley's agreed to pay £80,000 in 1896, only to discover that the barrelage was much less than indicated and many of the 90 pubs were on short leases or 'of little or no value'. After 20 years, Bythway had gained his revenge, though an offer of a place on Buckley's board was hastily withdrawn.

Having burnt its fingers, Buckley's was cautious about taking over another company, particularly since Carmarthen United Breweries had a troubled history. The caution paid off, since the price kept falling, until Buckley's bought the ailing concern for less than £50,000 in 1900.

It was now firmly established as the brewing giant of South-West Wales with more than 250 pubs.

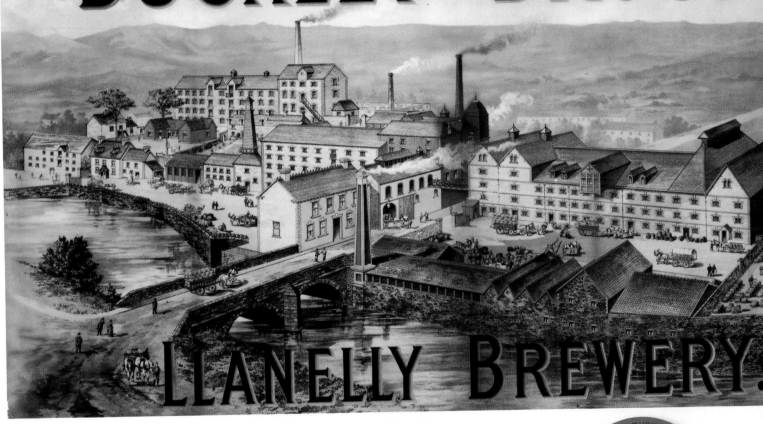

BUCKLEY BROS.

LLANELLY BREWERY.

A Buckley's 19th century poster shows the extent of the Llanelli Brewery, above, while a sketch from Barnard, top left, depicts one of the brewery yards.

BREWERS BY APPOINTMENT

Buckley's were the only brewery in Wales to gain the royal seal of approval – though no-one knows exactly why! The Royal Warrant was granted in 1903 by the Prince of Wales and Buckley's then became 'Brewers by Appointment to King George V' in 1910. The brewery may have supplied its beers to a function attended by the Prince in Wales, and he so enjoyed a glass or two that he allowed the brewery to use the royal coat of arms on its bottle labels and advertising.

Buckley Brothers did a large bottling trade in 1890. This was unusual at the time

Shining Pioneer

Buckley's might have been serving a very different area to city-centred Brains, but the range and mix of beers produced was remarkably similar – it also enjoyed a mighty dark mild trade.

At the end of March 1930, the brewing books show that out of a total of 46,310 barrels, XXX 6d Mild accounted for 36,924 barrels, almost 80 per cent of production. The next most popular beer was 6d Bitter Ale, with 4,518 barrels.

This is not surprising. Although Buckley's served a wide rural area, including seaside resorts like Tenby, the bulk of its beer sales were in heavy industrial towns like Llanelli and the surrounding mining villages.

What is surprising is that Buckley's for many years adopted a 'cleansing cask' system of final fermentation, similar to the 'unions' used by famous Burton brewers like Bass, which ensured a purer quality of beer. In 1904 Buckley's beer won the Champion Prize Gold Medal at the Brewers Exhibition in London, and took the Gold Medal for Ales and Stout at the Paris Exhibition in 1911. Between these victories it won silver medals three times. These successes help explain why Buckley's had been given a Royal Warrant in 1903.

What is also surprising is how early Buckley's broke into the bottled beer trade. When Barnard visited in 1890, he commented on the fact that Buckley Brothers 'do a large bottling trade'. This was unusual at the time. In 1930 flagons of Strong Ale were the brewery's third best-selling beer, accounting for 1,469 barrels, followed by its flagship bottled beer, Special Welsh Ale (844 barrels). In the late 1920s this brew was widely exported, notably to Argentina.

But if Buckley's had been a shining pioneer in glass, it was less certain about putting its beer into cans. And while it dithered, its local rival Felinfoel poured ahead to become the first British brewery to can beer, left.

The John family, who ran the Felinfoel Brewery, were also involved in the local tinplate industry. So in the dark years of the Depression, they had a vested interest in developing canned beer. While Buckley's investigated the possibility, Felinfoel dived into action in 1935.

On 3 December the *Llanelli and County Guardian* reported the historic moment under the triple heading, 'Canned Beer Arrives', 'Epoch-Making Process at Felinfoel Brewery' and 'New Hope for Tinplate Industry'. Buckley's was not amused at being beaten by its smaller neighbour. It took out adverts to proclaim: 'The canning of beer was accomplished at Buckley's Brewery bottling stores on the 3rd December, and samples may be seen at the brewery and at displays in the town. Until, however, the directors are satisfied that canned beer has the same estimable qualities as their bottled product, the process will be an experiment.'

There was a strong smell of sour beer.

Lt Col WH Buckley, centre on his horse, leads the New Year's Day hunt in Carmarthen in the 1950s.

PILLARS OF THE COMMUNITY

Like Brains in Cardiff, the Buckley family became prominent figures in their local community. One of the Buckley brothers who had formed the limited company in 1894, James Buckley, was High Sheriff for the county of Carmarthen. Like many brewing families, they also had close connections with the military. His nephew, Lieutenant Colonel William Howell Buckley, who became a brewery director in 1919 and chairman in 1948, was Assistant Provost Marshal in Malta during World War Two. But he was better known locally as master of fox hounds for the Carmarthenshire Hunt Society from 1932. He became High Sheriff of Carmarthenshire in 1950, as did his son Kemmis Buckley in 1967.

SHINING PIONEER

All that had been achieved began to crumble away

Boom and Bust

When Buckley's produced a booklet in the early 1980s about the brewery, chairman Lieutenant Colonel Kemmis Buckley, right, commented in the foreword, 'I often think that the main reason for our survival lies in the geographical position of our trading area. This is far enough to the west of Wales to have deterred large predator brewing companies in times past from making bids for us.'

However, after his retirement in 1983, Buckley's discovered there were no longer any safe hiding places. WIthout family succession, control passed outside the family, and all that had been achieved began to crumble away. For unlike many breweries, Buckley's had prospered after World War Two, with production rising from a low of less than 37,000 barrels in 1939 to around 60,000 during the 1950s and reaching more than 68,000 barrels in 1963. It was an impressive performance.

Best Bitter, a draught version of the bottled Special Welsh Ale, became the best-selling beer, accounting for half of production by the mid 1960s as mild declined. Tank beer was then introduced in

SCARLET FEVER

Buckley's always had close links with rugby. The brewery often helped Llanelli Rugby Club financially, and the club's headquarters were for many years in Buckley's Salutation Hotel in Church Street. 'Scarlet fever' reached such a thirsty pitch in 1972, after Llanelli beat the touring New Zealanders, that many pubs ran dry. 'Who beat the All Blacks? Good old Buckley's beers' was scrawled by regulars on a poster in one pub. The team celebrated again when Llanelli beat Australia in 1992, left.

1964, followed by keg beer from 1974, including the premium Buckley's Gold. Marketing was also brightened up with the adoption of a beer-drinking bardic figure in 1961, replacing Llanelli's 'Sospan Fach' and the Royal Coat of Arms.

When the brewery celebrated its 200th anniversary in 1967, it was a confident company, having invested heavily in the brewhouse and a new bottling plant, whilst the uneconomic maltings had closed in 1961. The Stripmill in Llanelli, opened in 1967, was fittingly its 200th pub. The brewery was further redeveloped in the early 1970s, ending the rolling of barrels across Gilbert Road which had regularly held up traffic in the city centre.

By 1975 turnover had topped £4 million. And in 1976 and 1981, two rights issues to shareholders, raising £1.75 million, allowed extra investment in the tied estate, including its first pub in Swansea city centre, The Builders Arms, in 1983.

But these issues meant more shares were on the market, and after Kemmis Buckley retired, with Griffith Phillips, a partner in a Cardiff stockbrokers, taking over as chairman, the company appeared increasingly vulnerable. Whitbread's share stake, which had looked reassuring in the 1960s, was now seen as a cause for concern.

Outsiders were soon prowling around. Tony Cole of property and finance group Bestwood built up a substantial share stake of 27 per cent from 1985. But blocked by Whitbread – he sold out in 1987 to another two financiers, Peter Clowes and Guy Von Cramer, who mounted a full bid for the company.

Buckley's branded the move most 'unwelcome', but when the offer was increased to £29 million in September 1987 the board felt bound to recommend it. They should have looked harder at the men behind the money.

Within less than a year, the Securities and Investment Board had made a liquidation order against Peter Clowes' gilt management company. When they defaulted on a loan to buy the brewery, corporate troubleshooters Morgan Grenfell were called in to sort out the mess.

Buckley's shares were suspended for 10 weeks and a loss of £763,000 was recorded for the last nine months of 1987. The brewery looked likely to close.

Then, in November 1988, a black knight rode to the rescue – accompanied by South Wales' remarkable United Clubs Brewery.

YOU CAN NAME A BIRD BY ITS SONG

You can recognise

CLUB BREWERY BEERS

By their Brightness, Purity and Palatability

1.—Can your Club afford to he p to pay for the losses on Brewery Tied Houses?

2.—Is there any reason why you should not take the advantage of the Value offered by the Clubs' Brewery?

Many Brewers charge our Clubs 5s or 6s, per barrel more than the Club Brewery prices.

3.—Does your Committee pay this higher price for any of your supplies?

4.—Can we convince you that our products are quite as good?

Our Beers are brewed from Pure Malt and Hops—no chemicals.

Most Clubs combine in Trade Unions and Co-operative Societies to protect their own interests. Why not support your own Brewery exclusively, and take the full advantage of Combined Trading?

Question—If you buy Club Brewery Beer 5s. per barrel cheaper than you are now buying other brewers beer, how much will your Club save in twelve months?

Answer— 1 barrel per week ... £13
2 barrels ... £26   5 barrels per week
3 ... £39   6 ... £65
4 ... £52   7 ... £78
8 ... £91
10 ... £104

Try it — Buy it — and don't be talked out of it.

SPEND WHERE YOU SAVE

This is not a private concern, but one controlled by Clubs and Clubmen only, for the benefit of the Clubs.

Bonus on purchases to all Clubs, whether Shareholders or not.

The South Wales and Monmouthshire United Clubs Brewery Co., Ltd.

THE CROWN BREWERY, BRYNSADLER, PONTYCLUN.

HALLETT & CO., 4f5, Mount Stuart Square, Cardiff.

Have another look at the first question above.

'Loyalty Pays' became
the slogan of the co-
operative venture.
The customer was king

Clubs United

In World War One, when beer supplies were severely limited, breweries naturally ensured their own pubs did not run dry. The many clubs in South Wales were not impressed with the poor service. They resolved to do something about it once the conflict was over.

A meeting of CIU clubs at the Cathays Liberal Club in Cardiff in March 1919, decided to form their own brewery. They wasted little time in setting the barrel rolling. In July they bought D&T Jenkins' Crown Brewery in Pontyclun for £20,000.

The business was ready-made for the clubmen, since the tall stone brewhouse on the road to the Rhondda already supplied many clubs in the mining valleys with XXXX Mild and Crown Pale Ale. The difference now was that the 61 CIU clubs were in charge, appointing the directors of the South Wales and Monmouthshire United Clubs Brewery, as it became known.

As well as directing the quality and price of the beer, the clubs also received discounts depending on the size of their shareholding and the amount of beer ordered. There were also seasonal bonuses and generous beer allowances. 'Loyalty Pays' became the slogan of the co-operative venture. The customer was king.

The established brewers poured scorn on this new scheme, claiming it would fail. In reality they feared this fresh competition, which undercut them on price. And they were right to be worried. For the clubs' trade was the main growth area in a depressed market as the number of clubs doubled between the wars, while the number of pubs declined. They also deeply resented the fact that clubs could open on a Sunday, while pubs were shut.

A delegate to a meeting of the South Wales Trade Defence League in 1927, under the chairmanship of W.H. Brain, said, 'In the old days people used to attend church and afterwards go into a public house for a glass of beer. Today they ignore the churches altogether and spend their Sundays in clubs.'

Business was so brisk that within a year, the share capital was increased to £50,000 to fund an expansion program at Pontyclun, with additional fermenting vessels added. Loans began to be made to clubs to help secure orders. By 1930 production was over 16,000 barrels a year. By 1940 trade had reached nearly 29,000 barrels.

The company blazed a trail for similar

ventures across Britain, with a delegation from the proposed West Midlands Clubs Brewery near Wolverhampton making a visit to Pontyclun in 1920. It also diversified into hotels, buying the Langland Bay Hotel near Swansea, above, in 1922 for the use of convalescing club members.

WARTIME SPIRIT

Despite the outbreak of war, the clubs' brewery adopted a 'business as usual' attitude, celebrating its 21st anniversary in 1940 with a souvenir booklet and a party for 300 at the Langland Bay Hotel in July. Days later reality hit home, as the café at the hotel was taken over by the military. Hitler's planes also blew up the board's plan for Christmas gifts to clubs, when the factory making tobacco pipes was bombed. Undeterred, the brewery ordered propelling pencils instead.

GONE FISHING

The Nant Felin Fach stream ran by the brewery and was for many years used to dispose of organic waste like excess yeast, cask washings and spent hops. This murky soup bred worms and other aquatic creatures – and these in turn attracted shoals of trout. Brewery workers found that setting night lines almost always resulted in catching a tasty fish or two. When modern regulations stopped waste disposal into the stream, the fish stopped biting.

Building Business

Demand did not slacken for the brewery's beers after the war. In fact, it soared from 28,674 barrels in 1940 to 38,170 a decade later. By 1954 it had reached 52,636 barrels, and the old stone brewhouse was literally creaking at the seams. With all the extra fermenting vessels added over the years, the walls were bulging. Tie-bars had to be added to prevent them collapsing under the strain.

With demand still rising, thanks to highly-competitive pricing, there was only one answer.

A completely new brewery would have to be built.

Some £90,000 was raised through new share issues to the clubs, while the Northern Clubs Federation Brewery of Newcastle loaned a similar amount to help build a modern brewery in the fields behind the old brewhouse. Though the first turf was cut in October 1951, post-war shortage of building materials meant the extensive steel, brick

and concrete complex was not completed until February 1954, with the first brew on 9 March.

With the new brewery capable of brewing more than 135,000 barrels a year, the future now looked bright, with vast scope for expansion. The company's reputation was also rising after a new brew, SBB (Special Best Bitter), introduced in 1958, won the championship for the best cask beer at the Brewers Exhibition in London just six years later. Eventually it accounted for a third of production.

From 1963 the brewery also introduced filtered tank beer delivered by large road tankers, right, and then piped directly into tanks in the cellars of larger clubs. For smaller outlets a pasteurised Crown Keg was added in 1970, followed by the stronger Sovereign.

By the time of its 50th anniversary in 1969, the clubs' brewery covered a great deal of South Wales, with a fleet of 20 lorries serving 300 clubs from Coleford in the east to Carmarthen in the west and as far as Brecon to the north.

The brewery was particularly proud of its contribution to the community. More than £3 million had been distributed to clubs in bonuses since the scheme began, allowing many to improve their premises. The chief guest at the 50th anniversary celebrations was the leader of the House of Commons, Fred Peart.

That year it also introduced a more striking identity, with the initials U.C. inside a crown. The brewery realised that it needed a sharper image to compete with the new national brewing groups, which were by then pushing hard for business in clubs by offering cheap loans and heavily marketing their beers.

The clubs' brewery also recognised that it needed to drive out of its heartland of the mining valleys into the major urban areas like Cardiff and Swansea, and even over the border into England, if it was to continue to thrive.

By its 50th anniversary in 1969, the clubs' brewery covered South Wales, with 20 lorries serving 300 clubs

As more and more clubs sought loans, finances were stretched to near breaking point

Uneasy Crown

The 1970s were to see two major changes, which completely altered the nature of the business – and at times unsettled it.

First the brewery ventured out of Wales, prompted by the collapse of the Midlands Clubs Brewery in 1969. By 1972 some 22 clubs in and around Birmingham were taking the beer. Later that year 400 club delegates attended tasting sessions in Cannock and Walsall, and club parties from the Midlands began to visit Pontyclun.

It was a bold move into a major new market, but it required substantial capital to sustain in the face of fierce competition from Ansells, part of Allied Breweries, and Mitchells & Butlers, part of Bass. An overdraft of £250,000 was agreed to finance the expansion, as more and more clubs sought

loans from the brewery. Finances were stretched to near breaking point.

The crunch came in 1975 when the Northern Clubs Federation Brewery of Newcastle suggested a joint venture to establish a depot in Coventry to supply the Midlands market. Crown would have to contribute £125,000. It was a step too far. The board turned down the offer and the Midlands trade trickled away as Federation took over on its own.

Instead, the board decided to break its exclusive links with clubs and start to market itself to a wider audience. This meant it began for the first time to sell its beer to pubs. It was a revolutionary change.

There was a new phrase on drinkers' lips – real ale. And the brewery still produced a substantial amount of cask beer. It was so traditional, it used oak casks and employed a cooper. When the fledgling Campaign for Real Ale in 1975 opened a pub in Bristol, The Old Fox, handpumped SBB was made a feature of the bar.

An advertising agency was appointed for the first time and the brewery began to sponsor rugby and horse racing. A new keg

beer, Great Western, was launched in 1976 backed by television advertising followed by the oddly-named 'Same Again', which was soon rebranded as Brenin Bitter.

The company was becoming more like other brewing companies. In 1975 it finally came in from the cold and when it joined the South Wales Brewers Association. And the following year, it dropped its dated title of the South Wales and Monmouthshire United

Gilfach Goch Social Club was one of many clubs in the Valleys to be substantially improved thanks to their links with the United Clubs Brewery.

Clubs Brewery to become simply Crown Brewery.

When chairman Penri Evans retired at the end of 1977, after 27 years' service, he was able to boast that turnover had increased from £250,000 in 1950 to £7.2 million in 1977. Annual production stood at almost 90,000 barrels. But Welsh clubs were still at the heart of the business, with three club visits to the brewery a week.

In 1979 the brewery extended its sales into West Wales by opening a depot in Narberth. Five years later it also opened a more daring depot in London.

The board also agreed to 'purchase a limited number of public houses' in 1979, but no progress was made until 1984 when the deepening recession meant a number of clubs went bust, leaving the brewery their premises.

It converted the Port Talbot Labour Club into a pub called St Oswalds and closer to home turned the Pontyclun Social Club into The Brunel Arms, left, in 1985. Financial support from Harp also allowed it to buy The Star Inn at Treoes, top left. It was to prove a significant link for the future.

WELSH LAGER

The brewery did not want to miss out on the growing lager market. In 1974 it became a partner in Guinness' Harp Lager venture. It was also eager to launch its own brand, and pondered marketing Federation's lager under its own name. In 1977 Crown considered a bolder scheme to brew a Welsh lager in conjunction with the other independent brewers in South Wales - Brains, Buckley and Felinfoel. But the ambitious plan failed to materialise.

It was a dangerous ambition, which toppled Crown's independence

Crown Buckley

When Clowes and Cramer's takeover of Buckley's of Llanelli fell apart in 1988, the company was put up for sale. Many brewing groups were reported to be interested, but no-one mentioned Crown.

But backed by Harp, and its parent company Guinness, the Pontyclun brewery was determined. In one major move, it would be able to gain a large pub estate. Like a secret military operation, it was called 'Project Yellow'. Perhaps red would have been a more appropriate colour. For it was a dangerous ambition, one which eventually toppled Crown's independence.

When Guinness announced in November that Harp had bought Buckley's for £25 million, it shocked the industry. Guinness had never previously been involved in running regional breweries or pub estates. But it was just seeking to expand its lager sales. Control of the 130 pubs was placed in a new company Crown Buckley Taverns, 75 per cent owned by Crown and the rest by Harp. Crown also gained the Llanelli brewery. Managing director Gareth Thomas described the combined business as 'the strongest independent brewery in South Wales'.

But it was clear one of the breweries would have to close. Crown was reluctant to axe the historic Llanelli site so it shut the Pontyclun brewhouse, while maintaining packaging there. It was a most unsatisfactory compromise, with beer having to be trunked miles between the two sites. Quality suffered.

The company was also heavily burdened with debt from the takeover. To be successful, business had to be brisk. A £500,000 advertising campaign was launched for Buckley's Best Bitter. But sales didn't soar. Instead, they plunged in the recession.

In 1989 Crown Buckley lost a massive £1,388,000. The Midland Bank threatened to withdraw its overdraft facilities. Only financial support from Guinness prevented bankruptcy, but control was slipping away. Losses continued. In September 1990 the stout giant stepped in and converted the heavy debt into a 75 per cent shareholding. Guinness was now in charge.

Mike Salter, a former finance director with Bass in Wales, was brought in as managing director. With a £7 million loan from Guinness, the business was stabilised, with the loss-making London depot closed and unprofitable pubs sold or closed. Sales began to rise, but not as fast as rumours about the future. Losses were still continuing, though at a lower level – £266,000 in 1992 – and Guinness was tiring of propping up the business. It wanted to pull out.

A management buyout, one of the largest ever made in Wales, was concluded in 1993 for the two sites and the beer business.

HISTORIC BREW

Crown Buckley's revival was helped by the launch in 1991 of a new premium cask beer The Rev. James, named after one of the Llanelli brewery's early owners, Methodist minister James Buckley. Head brewer Don Jeffrey, left, said it was based on a beer recipe from Buckley's 1885 brewing book. A special bottled brew of The Rev. James was produced to mark Buckley's 225th anniversary the following year.

Harp kept the 80 pubs, but Crown Buckley had first option to buy them. 'We have all had to put money in, and I am not entirely sure that our wives are happy about us securing our houses on the future of a brewery,' said Mike Salter, 'We are indulging in our dreams.'

The bold move paid off. Profits for the first 16 months were £1.46 million. Sales were helped by launching Buckley's Best as a nitrogenated 'smooth' keg beer and in 'widget' cans in 1995, followed by seasonal cask ales such as St David's and Merlin's Oak in 1996. New bottling and kegging lines were added at Pontyclun.

Although it had bought a handful of houses, buying the Buckley pub estate from Guinness proved more difficult. Only early in 1997 was it able to buy 28 houses around Swansea and Llanelli, with a further 27 to follow. But then the management buyout team led by Mike Salter decided to approach Brains, with a view to realising their capital. Shortly afterwards, an agreement was reached for Brains to acquire Crown Buckley.

Siân Lloyd, TV presenter on St David's Day 1996.

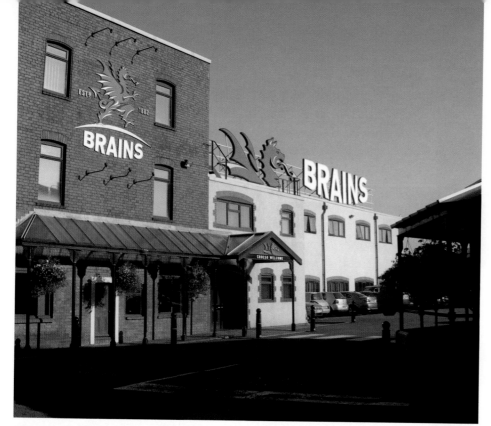

Christopher Brain, John Glazzard and Bill Rhys at The Old Brewery's final 'mash' in September 1999.

End of an Era

Brains moved quickly to put its name and dragon logo all over the former Hancock's brewery, including on the chimney, far right.

Brains takeover of Crown Buckley in February 1997 and the simultaneous announcement by Bass that it was to close its brewery in Cardiff in two years time, triggered volcanic changes in the brewing landscape in South Wales.

Like when Crown had merged with Buckley's, it soon became clear that one brewery would have to close, and this time there was no reprieve for Buckley's historic site in Llanelli. It closed early in 1998 and all Brains' brewing was concentrated in Cardiff.

What did come as a shock was Brains' announcement that it was about to close its own historic site and transfer production from the cramped Old Brewery in St Mary Street to the larger former Hancock's and Welsh Brewers' brewery behind Cardiff Central station, which Bass had put up for sale. Brewing had become increasingly difficult at the congested city centre Old Brewery site. It covered only 1.5 acres compared to Bass brewery's 8.5 acres.

Chairman Christopher Brain admitted, 'It will be a big wrench for me to leave these premises, but what we must do for our grandchildren is put the business in a position where it can be developed'. As part of the deal, Brains also took over Bass' depot in Maes-y-Coed Road, allowing it to close its distribution hub in Penarth Road.

And there were more significant changes to come. The retirement of Chief Executive Richard May-Hill and Managing Director Mike Salter, necessitated a restructure of the board. A New Chief Executive, Scott Waddington, was appointed in 2001 and a new vision for the company was agreed. Brains was set to become 'Wales' leading integrated, independent drinks and hospitality business, recognised by consumers and trade customers throughout the UK'.

The brewing and pub business was undergoing further consolidation and it was clear that Brains would have to increase the scale of its operation if it was to prosper. The consumer was also expecting more from a

"I thought they were closing —
I didn't know they were going to continue brewing just across the river."

visit to the pub, so the Brains estate had to evolve to offer a greater variety of offers and an increasing emphasis on food, customer choice and quality of service.

Growing and improving the quality of the pub estate was one of four cornerstones of the business plan identified by Scott Waddington, the others being developing the Brains brand, investing in Brains employees and meeting the licensed trade's needs through product range and service excellence.

Under the Chairmanship of Christopher Brain, a number of key board appointments were made over the first few years of the new Millennium. There was also an increased role for one of S.A. Brain's descendants, Great Great Grandson John Rhys (son of previous Chairman Bill Rhys), as Non-Executive Director and marketing consultant.

Brains was poised for one of the most exciting and dynamic periods of its 125-year history.

BUCKLEY BITES BACK

There was an unexpected twist in the tale when a member of the Buckley brewing family, Simon Buckley, who had established the small Tomos Watkin brewery at Llandeilo in 1995, launched an audacious £68m bid for Brains in February 1999, promising to continue brewing at The Old Brewery. He claimed to be backed by American money. But as larger predators had found in the past, the company was a tough nut to crack, with only 57 shareholders, most of them family members. The bid was unanimously and instantly rejected.

'This is an exciting development for Brains, as it combines our celebrated heritage with our dynamic future'

The former brewery tap, The Albert, below, was transformed into the Yard Bar & Kitchen, left.

Yards Ahead

The Old Brewery mashed its last beer in September 1999. But the buildings did not fall silent. There was to be a rousing send-off, a last booze-up in the brewery, when the yard was converted into a huge sporting venue with giant screens to watch the 1999 Rugby World Cup.

There was a special Arms Park Ale to mark the occasion and a bar 100 feet long manned by 30 staff, with speedy pint-

INTO SPACE

In 1996 bottles of SA, branded as Traditional Welsh Ale, were exported to the United States. The first consignment of 12,000 bottles went out in August to Boston. The following year draught beer followed, with the ale provided in kegs. In 1998 Brains travelled even further – into outer space. NASA astronaut Dr Dafydd Rhys Williams took a set of pump clip badges with him into orbit aboard the space shuttle Columbia. He later presented them to the brewery, left.

pouring machines. More than 50,000 pints were served to 15,000 fans over the six weeks of the tournament, below.

Then the developers moved in, with ambitious £25 million plans to create an impressive complex of shops, restaurants,

offices and apartments, to be known as The Old Brewery Quarter, including major names like Hard Rock Cafe, La Tasca and Nando's. Many of the 19th-century buildings were retained, with part of the cellars opened up to create a central sunken piazza.

As the venture neared completion in 2003, Brains and real estate investor Mansford Holdings combined to buy out the share of their joint developer, Countryside Properties, for £13 million. The brewer was developing a real taste for property beyond pubs.

Late in 2001, in combination with Mansford, it had also acquired the former Britvic depot in Llanishen, Cardiff, and moved its distribution operations there from Maes-y-Coed Road. The latter site was sold for housing, as was the former Crown Brewery in Pontyclun. Brains also gained planning permission to develop the Buckley's Brewery site in the centre of Llanelli.

On the Cardiff plans, Chief Executive Scott Waddington said, 'The transformation of The Old Brewery provides a significant

opportunity for our ambitious business. It is also a natural extension to the major investment we are making in the Yard Bar & Kitchen.' For part of the brewery yard had been combined with the brewery tap, The Albert, to establish the Yard Bar & Kitchen fronting The Old Brewery Quarter on St Mary Street. This striking flagship venue on two floors with three bars, opened in 2003. It was a bold exercise in brick, copper and steel. 'This is a exciting development for Brains as it combines our celebrated heritage with our dynamic future,' said Retail Director, Philip Lay.

Visitors to the 'Yard' and the surrounding development were not the only ones who were impressed. So was the building industry. Architects Powell Dobson picked up a string of awards, including a Gold Medal for Architecture at the National Eisteddfod in 2004, Best Leisure Regeneration Project at the Retail and Property Leisure Awards in 2005 and Best Mixed-Use Project at the Regeneration Awards the same year.

The Old Brewery had never been so busy.

Twelve girls at a revolving table could rattle out 240 dozen bottles an hour

Rail Ale

When Brains bought beer, wine and spirits wholesaler James Williams of Narberth in 2002, to strengthen its trade in West Wales, it tapped into one of the country's most remarkable drinks companies. The family links with beer ran deep, but its direct involvement with brewing was often troubled.

James Williams' inn sign at the Station House at Whitland emphasises the company's rail connections.

The original James Williams (there were three in total) was a farmer near Pembroke Dock, who, in 1827, decided to combine agriculture and ale to meet the thirsty demands of the growing port. He ordered a brewing copper from Bristol, but his ambitions outstripped his pocket and the following year he was imprisoned for debt.

However, two of his sons, Arthur and James, moved to Narberth, establishing a grocery and drapers business in the market square, which included a maltings to supply local publicans, most of whom still brewed their own beer. When the railway arrived in 1866, James Williams launched as a beer, wine and spirits merchant.

Perhaps deterred by his father's experience, he did not brew but ordered casks of ale by rail from the major Burton brewers instead. Much of the beer was bottled for local consumption. A stock book of 1897 shows the dominant supplier was Allsopp's.

Bottling became a major operation. The crown corking machine could cap

ELECTRIC DEVELOPMENT

The third James Williams, far left, was a bright spark. In 1900 to celebrate the relief of Mafeking, he set up an electric lamp standard outside the company offices, powered by a generating plant in Water Street. He went on to develop electric street lighting throughout the town, reputedly the first place in the area to see the light. Later he formed the Narberth, Pembroke and Haverfordwest Electrical Company.

Brains Chief Executive Scott Waddington, right, and Operations Director Jim Kerr take over the Narberth depot in 2002.

150 dozen bottles an hour. Hand labelling might have been expected to take longer, but 12 girls at a revolving table could rattle out 240 dozen an hour. The business even employed a basket maker to weave baskets for stoneware jugs.

When James Williams died in 1894 his son James took over, rapidly expanding the company by building a large bonded store in Church Street for spirits, including the firm's own Glomore Scotch and Doonmorey Irish whisky brands. He also substantially increased the small number of pubs owned by the business to more than 70. And with the arrival of the motor lorry in the 1920s, other depots were opened in Pembroke, Haverfordwest, Cardigan and Carmarthen.

The business had become the largest drinks wholesalers in South-West Wales. James Williams even briefly dallied with brewing again, taking over Pembroke Steam Brewery during World War One, to safeguard supplies during the conflict. But

this was a short-lived move and did not last long. Nor, sadly, did James Williams. He became depressed by the struggling trade in the late 1920s, and in 1930 he shot himself with a revolver. He was 63 and had never married.

The business continued as a limited company known as James Williams (Narberth) Ltd, first under the manager Mr A.E. Chadney until 1939, then under family relatives Hendrick Howell, followed in 1964 by John Lee-Davies.

By the 1980s the company had outgrown the cluster of old buildings around Market Square and moved to a more spacious, modern site in Spring Gardens, supplying its own 56 pubs and 600 free-trade customers.

Brains had links with the firm, having brewed a James Williams IPA for the Narberth company before the takeover. In July 2002, Brains bought the wholesale side of the business, along with its four depots and fleet of 20 lorries. Less than four months

later, the remaining 44 pubs were sold to Celtic Inns, which itself was later bought by Wolverhampton & Dudley Breweries, now trading as Marstons.

With the addition of another drinks wholesaler in 2003, Stedmans of Caerleon, near Newport, Brains had substantially strengthened its wholesale business across South Wales. And in June 2007 Brains ended the long connection with Narberth, by moving the hub of its West Wales operations to Whitland Green Business Park.

Bar Essential and Beyond

With the demise of Cardiff docks in the last quarter of the 20th Century, Brains could no longer rely on the Dark-drinking dock workers that had once been the backbone of their trade. The company had to develop its pub estate to offer the variety and quality demanded by the modern consumer.

The process had begun in the mid-1990s, when there were some dramatic additions to the Brains estate. One of the results was Bar Essential, which opened in Windsor Place in Cardiff late in 1997 (it is now simply known as 33 Windsor Place).

Places like Bar Essential were a mixture of café-bar and tavern. Further Bar Essentials were then opened in Bristol and Aberystwyth, while in Cardiff a larger bar restaurant called Inncognito, similar in style and décor, opened in a Victorian building in Park Place in 1999, with more than 2,000 square feet of bar and dining area.

Within a couple of months Brains had opened another addition to Cardiff's thriving café-bar scene in Wharton Street, with the even more intriguing name of 'Is it?'. The interior was equally striking, with a copper effect on the ceiling and bar, while wine displays were set into both the walls and the wooden floor, right.

'We do not want to lose our old market. Our core business of pubs is still predominantly community-based, and we do not want to change that,' said the brewery. 'But there is an opportunity to diversify our offering to the customer.

'We are being driven by the market and the market is about people, their aspirations and expectations. There is a new market. The new market is about food; it's about changing the way we operate and improving customer service.

'In the past quite a few of our pubs were predominantly male, some still are, but there

are fewer of them. They were places where women would not have gone, and the whole thing needs to change.'

But if traditional Brains drinkers popped into some of the company's new ventures, they would have been in for a shock. For these were bars, but not as they knew them. Brains were looking far beyond the Dark-drinking dock workers who had once been the backbone of their trade.

'The new market is about food; it's about changing the way we operate and improving customer service.'

QUAY DEVELOPMENTS

In 2003 Brains splashed out on two bars in Mermaid Quay at the heart of Cardiff Bay's stylish new waterfront. Both were oceans apart from the company's traditional community pubs. Bar 38 and Via Fossa were bought from Scottish & Newcastle, refurbished and reopened as Salt and Terra Nova (named after Captain Scott's ship which sailed from Cardiff on its final, fatal trip to the Antarctic). Both are contemporary two-storey bars, which have balconies overlooking the bay, and a strong emphasis on food and entertainment.

EZRA IRONSIDE

Brains in the late 1990s built up a small estate of around 10 pubs in the West Midlands. But rather than leaving the locals scratching their heads about the invasion of a brewery from South Wales called Brains, they rebadged them under the name of Ezra Ironside's Black Country Pub Company. The brand reflected the industrial background of many of the community pubs, such as The Boilermaker and The Chainmaker in Halesowen and The Nailmaker in Quarry Bank.

Pub Push

On 15 November 2000, the front page of the *Western Mail's* business supplement splashed the news that the brewery had received the backing of a consortium of banks led by Lloyds TSB.

The company was to embark on a significant drive to expand its estate over the next five to 10 years. The aim was not only to buy pubs in South and West Wales, but also in South-West England .

It was the most ambitious programme of growth ever announced by the business.

Brains' estate was already expanding. After the acquisition of Crown Buckley, which had added 28 pubs, Brains had acquired the remaining 23 Crown Buckley licensed premises from Guinness, taking its total up to 191 by the end of 1997. Further additions as far apart as Aberystwyth and Haverfordwest in the west to Monmouth and Crickhowell in the east pushed the number over 200 by the end of the century.

Food was becoming a significant and fast growing part of the business, with the emphasis on service onto a plate as well as into a pint pot.

But it was to prove difficult to rapidly increase the total estate, despite the financial backing at the brewery's disposal. Famous pubs were picked up, like the 15th-century Griffin Inn at Llyswen, near Brecon, in 2001, which was noted for its food, but it was piecemeal progress. By the time Brains bought four Beefeater pubs from Whitbread in June 2003, including The Pumphouse in Swansea Marina, right, the estate had edged up to 223.

A major advance came early in 2005 when Brains bought Innkeeper Wales of Cardigan, with its 27 pubs and hotels, which strengthened its presence in West Wales, particularly in popular town and seaside locations. This took the total estate to above 250, with the addition of 130 bedrooms. The

pubs included The Angel Hotel in Cardigan, The Ferry Inn at St Dogmaels, The Black Lion in Lampeter, The Harbour Inn, Solva, The Lord Nelson in Milford Haven and The Wellington Hotel in Brecon.

'This deal is strategically an excellent fit with our ambition to consolidate our position as the leading drinks and hospitality company in Wales,' said new chief executive Scott Waddington.

Since 2005, progress has been gradual with a number of excellent additions to the estate being secured, including the Plas Derwen in Abergavenny, the Piercefield in Chepstow and the Allensbank in Cardiff, which was reopened as the Grape & Olive in 2007.

The Watermill, Ogmore, above and top. The Harbour, Solva, right.

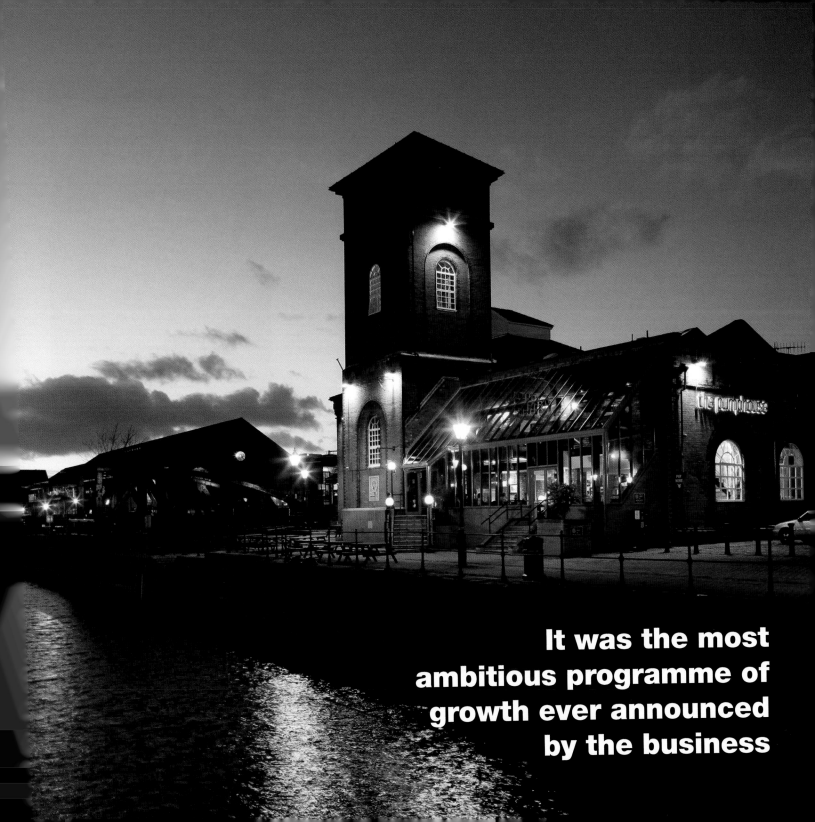

It was the most
ambitious programme of
growth ever announced
by the business

Fresh Brews

From the mid-1990s, Brains began to spice up its range, by adding a variety of new beers and seasonal ales to its classic mainstays of Brains Bitter, Dark and SA.

In 1995, Victory Ale celebrated the 50th anniversary of the end of World War Two in Europe. It was a strong 5% version of Dark, a reminder of how milds used to taste before beer's strength was sapped by two global conflicts.

To add to the nostalgia, Brains also produced special threepenny bits, which were given to customers every time they ordered a pint. Once drinkers had collected four, they could enjoy a pint for a shilling on VE Day. Victory Ale was also the official beer of the VE Day concert at Cardiff Castle on May 7.

A honeyed Summer Ale followed, creating another buzz at the bar, but Brains did not neglect their standard range. In fact, they expanded it in 1996. Nitrogenated 'smooth' versions of their popular Dark and Bitter were rolled out . This proved highly successful, sold under the slogan 'The Cool Alternative', with both winning medals at the Brewing Industry International Awards in 1998.

In 2004, an extra cold version of 'The Cool Alternative' followed promoted as 'Brrrrrains Smooth Extra Cold' in a TV advert, with 'BRRRR!' featuring on a poster campaign and at point of sale.

Brains had earlier turned to a famous Welsh poet – and drinker – for inspiration for a new premium brew. Dylan's was launched at the Dylan Thomas Centre in Swansea in April, 1998, with the poet's son and daughter, Llewellyn and Aeronwy, there to raise a glass. The opening lines of Under Milk Wood sighed across the back of the beer mats 'to the sloeblack, slow, black, crowblack, fishing-boat bobbing sea'. 'Dylan would have loved it,' said Aeronwy.

But despite pulling plenty of publicity and being relaunched as Dylan's Export in 2000, it slipped 'gentle into that good night' after failing to maintain its initial surge in sales.

But, by now Brains had established a taste for introducing new beers and continued to ring the changes. In April 2001, a seasonal ales range was launched, including a number of Buckley's former special brews, such as St David's Ale and Merlin's Oak, which have remained regular seasonals ever since.

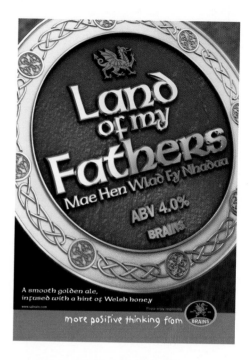

LAND OF MY FATHERS

In April 2006 Brains rolled out a limited edition ale to mark the 150th anniversary of the Welsh national anthem. Called Land Of My Fathers or Mae Hen Wlad Fy Nhadau, it commemorated Evan and James James who wrote the song in 1856. And as a tribute to the country's long brewing heritage, which includes mead and the spiced ale bragawd, the golden beer contained Welsh honey to help lubricate the many Welsh voices singing in celebration. Welsh ale was sparkling again.

Ringing the Changes

More recently the seasonal beer portfolio has been extended to include a Christmas Ale called Cwrw Seren (literally 'Star Ale'), Land of my Fathers, left, and a number of ales brewed to mark Brains rugby and cricket sponsorships.

But another more familiar ale was also making a name for itself – Brains Dark. Since ceasing to be the brewery's bread-and-butter brew, its unique flavour had attracted a growing band of admirers. In 2001 it was judged Champion Mild of Britain at CAMRA's Great British Beer Festival in London, before taking third place in the overall Supreme Champion Beer of Britain. In 2005 Dark Smooth won a gold medal at the Brewing Industry International Awards in Munich.

The following year Brains struck gold again when it launched a shining addition to its regular range of cask beers – SA Gold. The refreshingly hoppy golden ale, became Brains' strongest regularly-brewed draught beer at 4.7% ABV. In 2007, the quality of this new brew was recognised at CAMRA's Great British Beer Festival, where it won a Bronze Medal in the Champion Beer of Britain awards in the Strong Bitter Category.

SA SURPRISE

Brains SA mixed with more than the usual rugby crowd in 2000, when celebrity guests at the American wedding of Welsh actress Catherine Zeta-Jones and Michael Douglas (including UN Secretary General Kofi Annan, Russell Crowe, Sharon Stone and Steven Speilberg) were allegedly offered a choice of Perrier Jouet Champagne - or Brains SA. Skull Attack had become the Smart Alternative.

Positive Thinking

On joining the company in 2001, Scott Waddington, Brains' Chief Executive, had already identified the development of the Brains brand as a cornerstone of the new business plan. During 2002, Brains commenced a major rebranding process and marketing campaign, in which John Rhys, Great Great Grandson of S.A. Brain, played a leading role. The objective was to develop a new personality for the brand that would help raise its profile and develop a truly national identity. It was 'more positive thinking from Brains'.

The new brand positioning and slogan was introduced in February 2003, memorably linked to Welsh rugby with the scoreline that would be every positive thinking Wales supporter's dream splashed up on billboards all over South Wales: 'Wales 50: England 0'.

The rugby-themed billboards were followed in the summer with the company's first television advertising for six years. The most famous image of the the 'positive thinking' campaign that was featured on posters and in the TV commercial was a half-filled glass, showing the beer surreally in the top half of the glass, with the message 'always half full'.

Commented Scott Waddington, 'Brains' new campaign reflects the mood of optimism in Wales, which fits closely with our company's outlook on the future .'

The power of positive thinking was highlighted in a futher television advert in the autumn of 2003. It featured two hitch-hiking Welshmen optimistically writing their whole address in Pontypridd, down to flat number and postcode, on a piece of cardboard and standing at the roadside. Their positive thinking was rewarded by being given a lift to their door by two beautiful women in a stretched limousine.

It was a slogan with plenty of scope for fun outside sport, including an April Fool's Day joke in 2004 when adverts offered customers a new service – 'Brains on tap at home', showing a kitchen sink with an extra

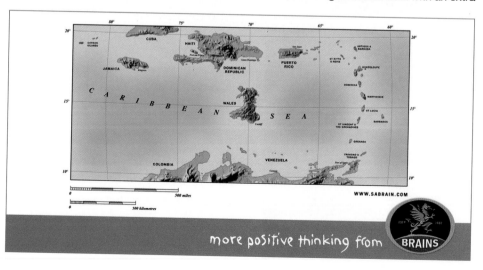

As part of the rebranding exercise, Brains changed its logo in 2003. It turned its dragon around, so that for the first time it was charging off to the right to give it a greater sense of forward momentum. It was also a more dynamic-looking beast, with sharper talons and tongue, confidently striding out into the future. The tentative step of the old dragon was gone.

tap for Brains Smooth between the hot and cold, above left. The offer was 'only available within a three mile radius of the brewery'. Customers were invited to call a hotline to get connected. Hundreds tried.

Other positive thinking posters included a map showing Wales moved to the warmth of the Caribbean in mid winter, left, and a 'Welcome to Wales' sign without the S and A in Wales, under the headline, 'It wouldn't be Wales without SA', right.

The campaign was such a striking success that Brains won several major awards for its marketing in 2005, including Marketing Strategy of the Year in the National Business Awards in competition with global names like Coca-Cola and Vodafone.

'This award is really the culmination of three years' work, beginning with a major research project among trade customers, consumers and staff that led us to our "More positive thinking from Brains" campaign,' said Sales and Marketing Director Richard Davies. With 'positive thinking' established, the future for Brains was looking very bright.

'Brains' new campaign reflects the mood of optimism in Wales'

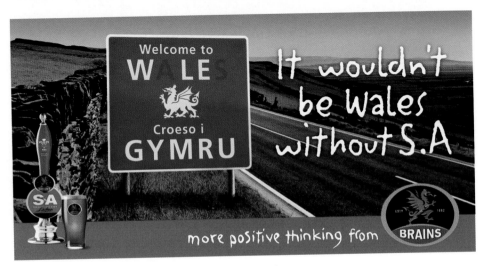

An inspired sponsorship that exceeded all expectations

Grand Slam

Brains has always had strong links with Welsh rugby. In 1996 it produced a stronger 5 per cent beer for the Five Nations tournament called Championship Ale, but it was only when it moved into The Cardiff Brewery in 1999 that it really put the rugby boot in.

That year, Brains announced a four-year sponsorship deal with Cardiff RFC. Arms Park Ale was produced on draught and in bottle, sporting the club's blue and black colours. Launched to coincide with the Rugby World Cup in Cardiff, it proved another winner for the company, taking a gold medal at the Brewing Industry

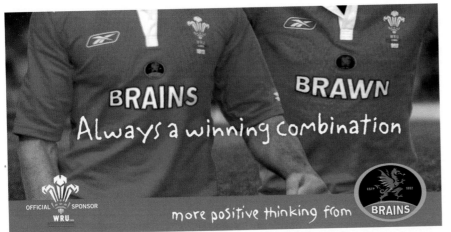

USING THEIR BRAWN

Brains had to use a neat sidestep to get round anti-alcohol advertising regulations in France. Instead of having Brains splattered across the national team's shirts, they switched to 'Brawn' for the crucial clash in Paris. It proved a winning move, as the Welsh muscled the French aside. In 2007 it repeated the trick with 'Brawn Again', establishing Brawn as the answer to sports trivia questions for years to come.

International Awards in 2000. It was also voted Rugby World Cup beer of the tournament by French sports paper *L'Equipe*.

Brains also began to sponsor rugby on television. In 2000 it put its name to S4C's *Y Clwb Rygbi* and HTV's *The Front Row*, giving it an enhanced presence on the Welsh rugby scene. But this was nothing compared to its next leap in the lineout.

In June 2004, Brains announced a major deal to have its name emblazoned across the famous red shirt of Wales. It was an ambitious move, and one matched by positive thinking about the national side. When the new strip was revealed in October, so was a poster featuring three members of the team under the claim, 'Official sponsor of the 2007 World Champions', left.

It was to be the first of many tongue-in-cheek rugby related adverts. One featuring Jonny Wilkinson trying to kick with his leg in plaster was withdrawn after the England outside half was injured. Another showing England's rose logo on a wooden spoon

(after England lost its first three matches in the 2005 Six Nations), above left, was ditched in case it upset the neighbours, but leaked out to become a popular email from

Welsh fans to rib their English friends. 'I can take it. I am not angry,' said former England captain Will Carling. 'It is all in good humour, I am sure.'

A special beer called Bread of Heaven was produced to mark the sponsorship and sold in distinctive tall bottles as well as on draught. It was a reddish colour, of course. And by the time the crunch Grand Slam match against Ireland arrived in March 2005, the brewery had installed striking new red pump handles featuring the WRU's three feathers logo in its city centre pubs.

On the match day itself, Brains sold more than a week's worth of beer in 24 hours as everyone celebrated. The inspired sponsorship exceeded all expectations, with huge demand for shirts and associated Brains merchandise.

'When we signed up for the sponsorship last summer, we could never have dreamed that the Welsh team would go on to have such a successful Six Nations,' said Group Marketing Manager Stewart Dobson. The national brewer of Wales had become a national icon.

J.H. Brain led Glamorgan to the Minor County Championship in 1900

Cricketing Legends

The Brain family were not only famous brewers, they also became local cricketing legends behind and in front of the stumps. And the long links with Glamorgan County Cricket Club, formed in 1888 at a meeting at the Angel Hotel in Cardiff, have been strengthened in recent years.

The cricketing connection goes back well over a century. Even Barnard in 1890 had his eye firmly on the ball, when he commented that J.H. Brain, the son of founder J.B. Brain, 'is the well-known and popular cricketer, who was captain of the Oxford team in 1887'. Joseph Hugh Brain

and his brother William Henry Brain, who were both later chairmen of the brewery, went on to play a major part in the development of Glamorgan, then struggling among the Minor Counties (full county status was not achieved until 1921).

Both became notable Glamorgan batsmen, William Brain scoring the club's first century in 1897. Oxford Blue Joseph had an even greater impact on the county. He often topped the averages, as well as keeping wicket and captaining the side.

He was also a major driving force on the county committee, threatening to resign in 1894 owing to his 'great disappointment at the apathy of players and the difficulty of putting a good team in the field'.

His words obviously stirred the side, as he led them to the Minor County Championship in 1900 and did not resign the captaincy until 1906, the year before he became chairman of the brewery. And he went out on a high, with 17 stumpings

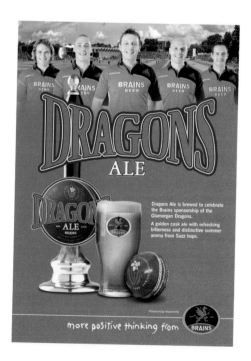

FAMOUS HAT TRICK

William Brain wrote his name into cricket's record books when, in 1893, he took the only first-class hat-trick by a wicket keeper, with three stumpings off three consecutive balls against Somerset. It is a record which has never been equalled. To mark the event and their sponsorship of Glamorgan in 2001, Brains produced a special beer called Hat Trick. Chairman Christopher Brain whipped the bails off the brew at the county ground alongside former captain Tony Lewis.

and 24 catches in 12 fixtures.

Brains linked up again with Glamorgan in 2001 when the brewery sponsored the county side, initially for three years. The relationship was extended for another 3 years in 2004. At first, players like Robert Croft and Matthew Maynard sported SA across their chests. Later the branding was changed to simply Brains Beer. The famous Brains name also featured on advertising boards around the grounds.

'As the national brewer of Wales, we place great emphasis on supporting Welsh sport,' said Group Marketing Manager Stewart Dobson.

Every season, Brains celebrated its sponsorship of Glamorgan with summer ales such as Taff End, above left, named after the eastern side of Glamorgan's Sophia Gardens ground in Cardiff, and Dragons Ale, left, derived from the one-day team's name.

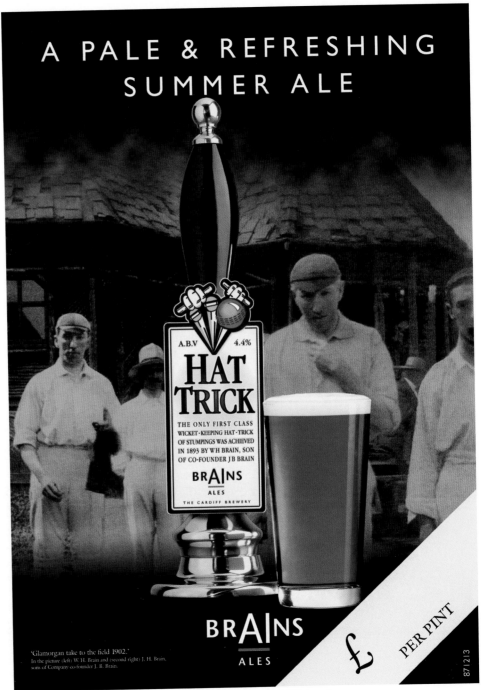

A PALE & REFRESHING SUMMER ALE

A.B.V 4.4%

HAT TRICK

THE ONLY FIRST CLASS WICKET-KEEPING HAT-TRICK OF STUMPINGS WAS ACHIEVED IN 1893 BY WH BRAIN, SON OF CO-FOUNDER J B BRAIN

BRAINS
ALES
THE CARDIFF BREWERY

BRAINS
ALES

£ PER PINT

'Glamorgan take to the field 1902.' In the picture (left) W. H. Brain and (second right) J. H. Brain, sons of Company co-founder J. B. Brain.

Both J.H. and W.H. Brain featured in the background photo in the Hat Trick poster.

The brewery's new 'continental' beer – 45 – became the official beer of Welsh football

OFFICIAL BEER OF WELSH FOOTBALL

Football Revolution

'Just imagine what would happen if we sponsored the football team too...' proclaimed a Brains advert in March 2005 after the rugby Grand Slam, beneath a scoreboard carrying the remarkable result, 'Wales 5: Brazil 1', below.

Eighteen months later this became a reality (the sponsorship, not the scoreline!), when Brains signed a two-year deal with the Football Association of Wales that saw the brewery's new 'continental-style' beer – 45 – become the official beer of Welsh football.

'The FAW is steeped in history and is the third oldest association in the world,' said Brains' Group Marketing Manager Stewart Dobson, 'So it is an honour and privilege for us to team up with them and complete our package of support for Welsh sport.'

But the beer advertised on billboards at the Millennium Stadium was totally up to date. In fact, the refreshing golden brew, served extra cold from flowing continental style fonts, was a revolutionary drop. Even the branded glasses were different, being laser-etched to create and hold the beer's head right to the last sip.

Designed to meet the increasing demand for continental style beer, 45 was described by Brains as 'a totally new concept for Welsh beer'. It was named after its alcohol strength

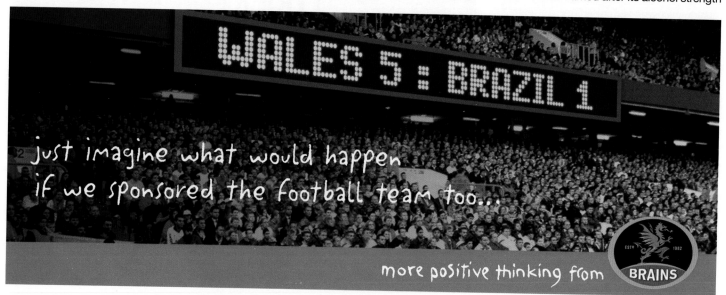

WALES 5 : BRAZIL 1

just imagine what would happen
if we sponsored the football team too...

more positive thinking from BRAINS

WALES IS GOING CONTINENTAL

BRRRR!

of 4.5 per cent. The matchday programme advert featured the headline: 'if you enjoyed the first 45, you'll enjoy the next 45 even more!'.

But 45 and the national team were far from Brains' only links with the round-ball game. One of the brewery's pubs became a shrine to Cardiff City. The Atlas in Canton was renamed the Ninian Park in 1927, to celebrate the club's famous FA Cup Final victory over Arsenal at Wembley.

The 112-year-old pub was demolished in 1978 for road widening, much to the disgust

of retiring licensee Billy Wheadon, below left, but the long relationship between pub and club was passed on to a new Ninian Park pub built 100 yards away down Leckwith Road – although City supporters had to wait a year for their first pint.

When the new pub, the Ninian Park, opened in 1979, it had the old, frosted glass window mounted behind the public bar and familiar photographs of Cardiff City teams on the walls. But everything else was different. The low brick and timber structure had a spacious, comfortable lounge and a small beer garden – ideal for children to kick a ball.

And Wales' latest young superstar, Gareth Bale, showed he had not forgotten his Cardiff roots when he celebrated his £10 million signing for Tottenham Hotspur in 2007 with, of course, a meal at his local Brains pub, The Fox & Hounds at Whitchurch.

ICE DEAL

Brains marked the launch of its Extra Cold Smooth in September 2005 with a cool new sporting deal. It sponsored the Cardiff Devils ice hockey team. The chilled ale, with its 'BRRRR!' slogan featured on the players' kit, as well as on perimeter advertising boards and on-ice branding at the Wales National Ice Rink in Cardiff. The refreshing new brew used Canadian Icefloe cooling technology to serve the chilled beer at three degrees, as a way of retaining drinkers in the ale category during the warmer summer months.

Brains has not only survived but prospered. Stylish new bars, beers and marketing have blown away the old industrial image

National Champions

In recent years many traditional British family brewers have struggled in the face of fierce competition. Many have disappeared. Familiar local breweries like King & Barnes of Sussex, Gales of Hampshire and Hardy & Hanson of Nottingham have been taken over and closed down.

Brains has not only survived, it has prospered. Instead of going on the defensive it has expanded, moving to a much larger brewery and greatly increasing the size of its tied estate. Stylish bars, new beers and innovative marketing have blown away the old industrial image, while the ambitious sponsorship of Welsh sport made Brains the indisputable national beer of Wales, as inextricably linked with the country as Guinness with Ireland.

The world began to sit up at the bar and take note. In 2003, Brains was crowned Welsh Company of the Year in the Western Mail Business Awards. In 2004, the Cardiff-based brewer smashed through the £100 million turnover barrier for the first time to reach £108 million. It was the fifth consecutive year of growth, built on a progressive buisness plan.

In 2005 it was named Regional Brewer of the Year in the annual awards organised by trade magazine *The Publican,* as well as winning The National Business Awards Marketing Strategy of the Year. The judges said the company had an 'amazingly good understanding of the market place'. Production that year reached almost 100,000 barrels, with sales increasing in a declining market.

When Brains launched Champions Ale early in 2006, to celebrate the Welsh rugby team's Grand Slam success the previous year, it could also have been a tribute to its own performance. There was more positive news from Brains when it announced its results for 2005, with turnover up again

to more than £120 million. Chief Executive Scott Waddington said, 'The Brains brand is very rapidly becoming identified as the leading Welsh beer brand and sales of our ales continue to increase in a declining market.' He added, 'We are also particularly pleased to see the company winning so many awards.'

And the awards kept flowing in. Brains was named Managed Pub Company of the Year in the 2006 Publican Awards. It also won the Marketing Society's Brand Revitalisation Award that year.

Brains was making everyone sit up, take notice and wonder what it could achieve in the next 125 years.

Key Dates

1713: Founded as a pub brewhouse.

1813: First common brewer, James Walters, recorded as brewing.

1844: William and Charles Andrews first to call the site The Old Brewery.

1862: John Thomas buys the brewery for his sons.

1863: Samuel Arthur Brain arrives in Cardiff, aged 12.

1872: Marries John Thomas' daughter Frances Elizabeth.

1882: With his uncle Joseph Benjamin Brain of Bristol, Samual Arthur Brain buys The Old Brewery from Edward Thomas.

1885: S.A. Brain elected to Cardiff Council.

1886: S.A. Brain becomes one of the founders of the Cardiff Malting Company.

1887: Builds much larger and grander brewhouse on The Old Brewery site.

1897: A limited company, S.A. Brain & Company Ltd., formed.

1899: S.A. Brain becomes Mayor of Cardiff.

1903: S.A. Brain dies. His uncle, Joseph Benjamin Brain, takes over as chairman.

1907: J.B. Brain dies and his son, Joseph Hugh Brain, takes over.

1914: Work starts on building The New Brewery in Roath to produce bottled beer.

1914: J.H. Brain dies and his brother, William Henry Brain, takes over.

1919: New Brewery completed; original small brewery behind The Albert demolished.

1921: W.S. Sweet-Escott, who had married S.A. Brain's daughter Ethel, takes over as chairman for five years.

1934: W.H. Brain dies and H.H. Sweet-Escott takes over.

1955: W.H. Brain's son, Michael Benjamin Brain, becomes chairman.

1956: Brains takes over five Cardiff pubs run by wine merchants Greenwood and Brown.

1971: M.B. Brain dies and S.A. Brain's Great Grandson, Bill Rhys, takes over as chairman.

1976-82: The Old Brewery is modernised and expanded.

1984: First marketing department set up.

1989: M.B. Brain's son, Christopher Brain, takes over as chairman from Bill Rhys.

1993: The New Brewery in Roath closes.

1997: Brains acquires Crown Buckley of Llanelli and Pontyclun.

1999: The Old Brewery closes and production moves to the former Hancock's brewery in Cardiff, which was bought from Bass.

2000: Brains launches major drive to buy pubs with £50m war chest.

2002: Takes over beer wholesalers James Williams of Narberth.

2003: Launches 'More Positive Thinking' advertising campaign.

2003: Named Welsh Company of the Year in the Western Mail Business Awards.

2004: Announces sponsorship of the Welsh rugby team.

2005: Wales win the Grand Slam!

2005: Acquisition of Innkeeper Wales' 27 pubs to take its estate to over 250 houses.

2006: New 'continental' beer, 45, becomes Official Beer of Welsh Football.

2007: 125th anniversary.

Brains Chairmen 1897–2007

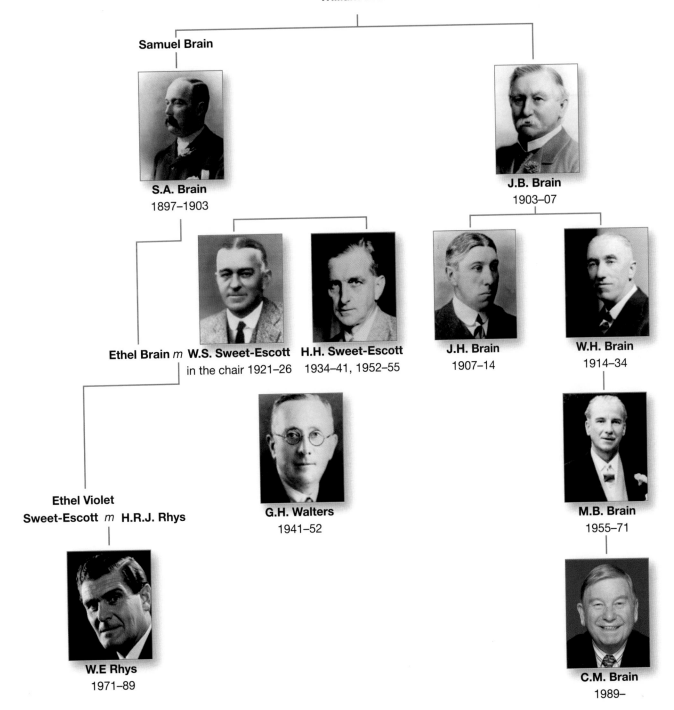

William Brain

Samuel Brain

S.A. Brain
1897–1903

J.B. Brain
1903–07

Ethel Brain *m* **W.S. Sweet-Escott**
in the chair 1921–26

H.H. Sweet-Escott
1934–41, 1952–55

J.H. Brain
1907–14

W.H. Brain
1914–34

**Ethel Violet
Sweet-Escott** *m* **H.R.J. Rhys**

G.H. Walters
1941–52

M.B. Brain
1955–71

W.E Rhys
1971–89

C.M. Brain
1989–

Pub List

Name	Address	Town	Postcode
33 Windsor Place	33 Windsor Place	Cardiff	CF10 3BZ
Abergwaun	Market Street	Fishguard	SA65 9HA
Abertawe Alehouse	296 Oystermouth Road	Swansea	SA1 3UJ
Adam & Eve	207 High Street	Swansea	SA1 1PE
Admiral Napier	239 Cowbridge Road East	Canton	CF11 9AL
Albany	105 Donald Street	Roath	CF24 4TL
Albion	28 Glebe Street	Penarth	CF64 1EF
Alma	5 Priory Street	Milford Haven	SA73 2AD
Ancient Briton	1 Clevis Hill	Newton	CF36 5NT
Angel Hotel	36/37 St Mary's Street	Cardigan	SA43 1DH
Angel Hotel	43 High Street	Narberth	SA67 7AS
Aubrey Arms	Swansea Road	Bonvilston	CF5 6TQ
Bar Billabong	Wellfield Road	Roath	CF24 3PE
Bar Charlie	1-2 Dark Street	Haverfordwest	SA61 2DS
Bar Essential	Portland Street	Aberystwyth	SY23 2DX
Bar Number One	1 The Bulwark	Brecon	LD3 7LB
Barfly	Kingsway	Cardiff	CF10 1ED
Baroness Windsor	170 Penarth Road	Cardiff	CF11 6NL
Bay Hotel	35/37 Marine Terrace	Aberystwyth	SY23 2BX
Beaufort Arms	18 Pennard Road	Kittle	SA3 3JB
Birchgrove	Caerphilly Road	Birchgrove	CF14 4AE
Black Boy	444 Gower Road	Killay	SA2 7AJ
Black Horse	Iscoed Road	Pontardulias	SA4 0UN
Black Lion	High Street	Lampeter	SA48 7BG
Black Lion	49 Cardiff Road	Llandaff	CF5 2DQ
Black Lion	Llanrhystud	Llanrhystud	SY23 5DG
Blackweir Tavern	North Road	Cardiff	CF10 3DX
Blinkin Owl	Henllys Way	Cwmbran	NP44 4TP
Bluebell	Glangrwyney	Nr Crickhowell	NP8 1EH
Boathouse	Newbridge Road	Bath	BA1 3NB
Brains Surgery	36/37 Daffod St	Bath	BA1 6SW
Brunel Arms	Station Approach	Pontyclun	CF72 9DS
Builders Arms	36 Oxford Street	Swansea	SA1 3HT
Burgess Green	Ysguthan Road	Aberavon	SA12 6NB
Butchers	29 Llandaff Road	Canton	CF11 9NG
Canadian Hotel	143 Pearl Street	Roath	CF24 1PN
Canton	6 Llandaff Road	Canton	CF11 9NG
Cardiff Arms	63 Railway Street	Splott	CF24 2DF
Castle	Jewel Street	Barry	CF63 3NQ
Castle	High Street	Lampeter	SA48 7BG
Chainmaker	130 Colley Lane	Halesowen	B63 2BX
Church House	Church Road	St. Brides Wentlooge	NP10 8SN
Church Tavern	36 High Street	Quarry Bank	DY5 2AA
Churchills Hotel	Cardiff Road	Llandaff	CF5 2AD
City Arms	10/12 Quay Street	Cardiff	CF10 1EA
Clifton	1 Clifton Street	Roath	CF24 1PW
Coach & Horses	Welsh Sreet	Chepstow	NP6 5LN
Cockett Inn	Waunarlwydd Road	Sketty	SA2 0GB
Colliers Arms	52 Bridgend Road	Aberkenfig	CF32 9BA
Commercial Hotel	Station Road	Gowerton	SA4 3AJ
Coopers Arms	Neath Road	Plasmarl	SA6 8JU
Cornwall	92 Cornwall St	Grangetown	CF11 6SR
Cottage	25 St Mary Street	Cardiff	CF10 1AA
Court Royale	21 Eastgate Street	Aberystwyth	SY23 2AR
Cross Inn	783 Newport Road	Rumney	CF3 4AJ
Cross Keys	70 Glebe Road	Loughor	SA4 6SR
Crown	North Street	Rhayader	LD6 5BT
Crown	216 New Road	Skewen	SA10 6EW
Crown Inn	High Street	Staple Hill	BS16 5HP
Crown Inn	Lower Frog Street	Tenby	SA70 7HU
Crwys	34 Crwys Road	Cathays	CF24 4NN
Culverhouse	427 Cowbridge Road West	Ely	CF5 5TF
Cwm Talwg	Severn Avenue	Barry	CF62 7JL
Darran	2 St Mary Street	Risca	NP11 6GU
Dempseys	15 Castle Street	Cardiff	CF10 1BS
Dolau	Church Street	New Quay	SA45 9NT
Duke Of Clarence	48 Clive Road	Canton	CF5 1HJ
Duke Of Wellington	48 High Street	Cowbridge	CF71 7AG
Encore	11 Denmark Street	Bristol	BS1 5DQ

Name	Address	Town	Postcode
Fairwater	St Fagans Road	Fairwater	CF5 3AH
Fairwater R.F.C.	Plasmawr Road	Fairwater	CF5 3JX
Farmers Arms	Waunarlwydd	Swansea	SA5 4SL
Ferry Inn	Poppit Road	St Dogmaels	SA43 3LF
Fishguard Arms	47 Old Bridge	Haverfordwest	SA61 2EZ
Flora	136 Cathays Terrace	Cathays	CF24 4HY
Forge	11 Dudley Road	Halesowen	B63 3LS
Fountain Inn	12 Woodfield Street	Morriston	SA6 8AQ
Fox & Hounds	Chapel Row	St. Mellons	CF3 5UB
Fox & Hounds	Old Church Road	Whitchurch	CF14 1AD
Full Moon Inn	22 The Parade	Neath	SA11 1RA
Galleon Inn	35 Enfield Road	Broad Haven	SA62 3JN
Goat Major	33 High Street	Cardiff	CF10 1PU
Golden Cross	282 Hayes Bridge Road	Cardiff	CF10 1GH
Golden Grove	Llanarthney	Carmarthen	SA32 8JU
Gower	Gwennyth Street	Cathays	CF24 4PH
Grange	134 Penarth Road	Grangetown	CF11 6NJ
Grape	24 St. Marys Street	Chepstow	NP16 5EU
Grape & Olive	49 Wedal Road	Heath	CF14 3QX
Grasshoppers	St. Johns Street	Abergavenny	NP7 5RT
Great Western	47 Station Road	Ammanford	SA18 2DB
Green Dragon	Llancadle	Nr Barry	CF62 3AQ
Greenfields	Erw Road	Llanelli	SA15 1TE
Greenhouse	Newport Road	Llantarnam	NP44 3BP
Griffin	Llyswen	Brecon	LD3 0UR
Grosvenor	South Park Road	Splott	CF24 2LU
Grove Hotel	High Street	St Davids	SA62 6SB
Gwesty Bach	Clarence Street	Brynmawr	NP23 4EH
Half Moon	71 Wern Road	Llanelli	SA15 1SP
Halfway	247 Cathedral Road	Pontcanna	CF11 9PP
Hanbury Ale House	Uskside	Caerleon	NP18 1AA
Harbour Inn	31 Main Street	Solva	SA62 6UT
Heart Of Oak	47/49 Newtown Road	Hereford	HR4 9LJ
Heath	Whitchurch Road	Heath	CF14 3LW
Hen & Chickens	Flannel Street	Abergavenny	NP7 5EG
Hendre	Hendre Road	Trowbridge	CF3 1ST
Highfields	Caerau Road	Ely	CF5 5JP
Hollybush	Glyn Coed Road	Llanedeyrn	CF23 7DX
Hope & Anchor	51 Pendre	Cardigan	SA43 1JS
Horseshoe	Beaufort Road	Llangattock	NP8 1PA
Imperial	1125 Neath Road	Plasmarl	SA6 8JW
Inncognito	29 Park Place	Cardiff	CF10 3BA
Insole Arms	16 Harvey Street	Canton	CF5 1QW
Is it?	12 Wharton Street	Cardiff	CF10 1AG
Joiners Arms	58 Llwynhendy Road	Llanelli	SA14 9HR
Jolly Sailor	Church Street	Newton	CF36 5PD
Kavanaghs	2 Queen Victoria Road	Llanelli	SA15 2TL
King of Prussia	Penpergwm	Nr Abergavenny	NP7 9AR
Kings Arms	Church Road	Pentyrch	CF15 9QF
Kings Head	East Street	Llantwit Major	CF61 1XY
Kitty Flynn's	51 St Mary Street	Cardiff	CF10 2AD
Lamb & Flag	Brecon Road	Abergavenny	NP7 7EW
Lamb Inn	12 Broad Street	Builth Wells	LD2 3DT
Langford Inn	Lower Langford	Langford	BS40 5BL
Lantern	Bethesda Street	Merthyr Tydfil	CF47 8LN
Lewis Arms	Mill Road	Tongwynlais	CF15 7JP
Lighthouse	153 Coombs Road	Halesowen	B62 8AF
Lord Beeching	Alexandra Road	Aberystwyth	SY23 1LE
Lord Nelson	Hamilton Terrace	Milford Haven	SA73 3AW
Mallards	High Street	Midsomer Norton	BA3 2DR
Malt Shovel	61 High Street	Rolley Regis	B65 0EH
Maltsters	Cardiff Road	Llandaff	CF5 2DS
Maltsters	75 Merthyr Road	Whitchurch	CF14 1DD
Mardy Hotel	117 High Street	Gorseinon	SA4 2BT
Marine	Redbrink Crescent	Barry Island	CF62 5TT
Master Mariner	Skomer Road	Gibbonsdown	CF61 3DA
Merrie Harrier	Penlan Road	Llandough	CF64 2NY
Mitre	Wyndham Street	Canton	CF11 6DQ
Model Inn	14/15 Quay Street	Cardiff	CF10 1EA
Monachty	Market Street	Aberaeron	SA46 0AS

Name	Address	Town	Postcode
Nags Head	34 Market Place	Great Bridge	DY4 7EJ
Newbridge	Abergele Road	Trowbridge	CF3 1RR
New Dock Tavern	188 Broadway	Roath	CF24 1QJ
New King George	123 Priory Street	Carmarthen	SA31 1NB
Ninian Park	Leckwith Road	Canton	CF11 8HH
O'Briens Exchange	10 The Strand	Swansea	SA1 2AE
Old Arcade	14 Church Street	Cardiff	CF10 1BG
Old Cross Inn	Quay Street	Ammanford	SA18 3DB
Old Flower Pot	High Street	Kingswood	BS15 4AQ
Old Inn	Swansea Road	Penllergaer	SA4 9AQ
Old Nags Head	Granville St	Monmouth	NP25 3DR
Old Post	Swansea Road	Bonvilston	CF5 6TQ
Old Station	Wells Road	Hallatrow	BS39 6EN
Packet	95 Bute Street	Cardiff Bay	CF10 6AB
Park	Park Crescent	Barry	CF62 6HE
Park	Station Road	Ebbw Vale	NP23 6TN
Pemberton Arms	Colby Road	Burryport	SA16 ORH
Pendragon	Excalibur Drive	Thornhill	CF14 9BB
Penwig	South John Street	Newquay	SA45 9NN
Perrivale Inn	89 Portamman Road	Ammanford	SA18 2JD
Pheasant	Heol Eglwys	Pen-y-Fai	CF31 4LY
Phoenix	1 Penygroes	Gorslas	SA14 7LA
Pick & Shovel	Fothergill Street	Treforest	CF37 1SG
Piercefield	St Arvans	Chepstow	NP16 6EJ
Pilot	67 Queen's Road	Penarth	CF64 1DJ
Pineapple	37 St Georges Road	Bristol	BS1 5UU
Plas Derwen	Monmouth Road	Abergavenny	NP7 9SP
Plough	1 Merthyr Road	Whitchurch	CF14 1DA
Plume Of Feathers	St Mary's Street	Carmarthen	SA31 1TN
Pontygwindy	Pontygwindy Road	Caerphilly	CF83 3HR
Pump House	Pump House Quay	Swansea	SA1 1TT
Punch House	Agincourt Square	Monmouth	NP25 3BT
Railway	144 Ely Road	Llandaff	CF5 3AB
Railway Tavern	Dukestown Road	Tredegar	NP22 4QD
Red Cow Inn	Llandybie	Ammanford	SA18 3JA
Red Dragon	Litchard Hill	Bridgend	CF31 1QJ
Red Lion	Bonvilston	Bonvilston	CF5 6TR
Red Lion	St. Mary Street	Cardigan	SA43 1DD
Retreat	Maelfa	Llanedeyrn	CF23 9PL
Reverend James	180 Borough Road	Loughor	SA4 6RL
Roath Cottage	25 Plasnewydd Road	Roath	CF24 3EN
Roath Park	170 City Road	Roath	CF24 3JE
Romilly	69/71 Romilly Crescent	Canton	CF11 9NQ
Rompney Castle	Wentloog Road	Rumney	CF3 3AB
Rose & Crown	Eglwysilan	Abertridwr	CF83 4JG
Royal Exchange	Ty Mawr Road	Llandaff North	CF14 2FQ
Royal Oak	Market Square	Fishguard	SA65 9HB
Royal Oak	200 Broadway	Roath	CF24 1QJ
Rumpoles	Adam Street	Adamsdown	CF10 2FH
Salt	Mermaid Quay	Cardiff Bay	CF10 5BW
Salt @ The George	706 Mumbles Road	Mumbles	SA3 4EH
Savoy Country Inn	Tenby Road	St. Clears	SA33 4JP
Sawyers Arms	5 Commercial Street	Maesteg	CF34 9DF
Scholars	10 Queens Road	Aberystwyth	SY23 2HH
Seagull	Sandpiper Road	Porthcawl	CF36 3UT
Ship	1 Pendre	Cardigan	SA43 1JL
Ship Aground	123 Ashburnham Road	Pembrey	SA16 OTL
Ship Inn	Tresaith	Cardigan	SA43 2JL
Smiths Arms	1 Pontardulais Road	Llangennech	SA14 8YE
Smiths Arms	38 Gelli Road	Penceiliogi	SA14 9AA
Smoking Dog	62 High Street	Malmesbury	SN16 9AT
Splotlands	Meteor Street	Splott	CF24 0HW
Sporting Chance	Red Roses	Llanteg	SA34 0PD
Stag	Five Roads	Llanelli	SA15 5YR
Star	Station Road	Dinas Powys	CF64 4DE
Star Inn	Treoes	Nr Bridgend	CF35 5DL
Station	162 Windsor Road	Cogan	CF64 1JG
Stradey Arms	1 Stradey Road	Llanelli	SA15 4ET
Swan	213 Cardiff Road	Dinas Powys	CF64 4JW
Sycamore Tree	Coed Masarnen	Colwinston	CF71 7NG
Tafarn Tanerdy	Penlanffos Road	Carmarthen	SA31 2EY
Tafarn y Trapp	Swansea Road	Gorseinon	SA4 2AS
Talbot Inn	Pwll Road	Pwll	SA15 4AP

Tanners Arms	Barn Road	Carmarthen	SA31 1QU
Tavistock	Bedford Street	Roath	CF24 3DB
Terra Nova	Mermaid Quay	Cardiff Bay	CF10 5BZ
Thomas Arms Hotel	Thomas Street	Llanelli	SA15 3JF
Three Arches	Heathwood Road	Heath	CF14 4HS
Three Compasses	Sycamore Street	Newcastle Emlyn	SA38 9AJ
Three Horse Shoes	Merthyr Road	Gabalfa	CF14 1DL
Three Horse Shoes	Church Lane	Peterston-Super-Ely	CF5 6LH
Three Horse Shoes	Corn Square	Leominster	HR6 8LR
Three Salmons	5 Water Street	Carmarthen	SA31 1PY
Three Sisters	Mansel Terrace	Cwmbwrla	SA5 8NN
Tollgate	Piercefield Lane	Aberystwyth	SY23 1RX
Travellers Well	554 Carmarthen Road	Cwmdu	SA5 8LA
Treacle Mine	83/85 St Martins Street	Hereford	HR2 7RG
Treorchy Hotel	165 Bute Street	Treorchy	CF42 6DA
Twelve Knights	Margam Road	Port Talbot	SA13 2DB
Two Brewers	Brackla Way	Brackla	CF31 2AR
Ty Mawr	Graig Road	Lisvane	CF14 0UF
Tynant	Tynant Road	Morganstown	CF15 8LB
Tynewydd	Tynewydd Road	Barry	CF62 8BB
Ty-Risha	Pen-y-Cae	Bridgend	CF32 9SN
Victoria Park	422 Cowbridge Road East	Canton	CF5 1JL
Vivian	104 Gower Road	Sketty	SA2 9BZ
Vulcan	10 Adam Street	Adamsdown	CF24 2FH

Waggon & Horses	17a Church Street	Oldbury	B69 3AD
Watermans Arms	2 The Green	Pembroke	SA71 4NU
Watermill	Ogmore Road	Ogmore by Sea	CF32 0QP
Welcome To Gower	2 Mount Sreet	Gowerton	SA4 3EJ
Wellington Hotel	The Bulwark	Brecon	LD3 7AD
Wellingtons	42 The Hayes	Cardiff	CF10 1AJ
Wenvoe Arms	18 Old Port Road	Wenvoe	CF5 6AN
Westgate	49 Cowbridge Road East	Riverside	CF11 9AD
Wharf	Atlantic Wharf	Cardiff Bay	CF10 4EU
White Hart	Brecon Road	Crickhowell	NP8 1DL
White Hart	66 James Street	Cardiff Bay	CF10 6EZ
White Horse	Buckover	Wootton-under-Edge	GL12 8DX
White Horse	Coychurch	Bridgend	CF35 5HD
White Horse Inn	Pembrey Road	Llanelli	SA15 3BP
White Lion	60 Pemberton Road	Llanelli	SA15 2HH
Willows	Willowbrook Drive	St. Mellons	CF3 9YG
Windsor	170 Holton Road	Barry	CF63 4HL
Windsor	95 Windsor Road	Penarth	CF64 1JE
Wolf's Castle	Templeton Avenue	Llanishen	CF14 5JS
Wolfe Inn	Wolf's Castle	Haverfordwest	SA62 5LS
Y Draenog	Cowbridge Road	Brynsadler	CF72 9BT
Yard	42/43 St Mary Street	Cardiff	CF10 1AD
Ynyscedwyn Arms	53 Commercial Street	Ystradgynlais	SA9 1LA